Shiny Shoes on Dusty Paths

The Polishing of Grace

As told to
Joanne Kroeker

Treasure House

An Imprint of
Destiny Image Publishers, Inc.®
P.O. Box 310
Shippensburg, PA 17257-0310

"For where your treasure is
there will your heart be also." Matthew 6:21

ISBN 1-56043-845-2

For Worldwide Distribution
Printed in the U.S.A.

Treasure House books are available through these fine distributors outside the United States:

Christian Growth, Inc.,
Jalan Kilang-Timor, Singapore 0315

Rhema Ministries Trading
Randburg, South Africa

Salvation Book Centre
Petaling, Jaya, Malaysia

Successful Christian Living
Capetown, Rep. of South Africa

Vine Christian Centre
Mid Glamorgan, Wales, United Kingdom

Vision Resources
Ponsonby, Auckland, New Zealand

WA Buchanan Company
Geebung, Queensland, Australia

Word Alive
Niverville, Manitoba, Canada

Inside the U.S., call toll free to order:
1-800-722-6774

Acknowledgments

With a sense of indebtedness I acknowledge profound gratitude to the many people who contributed in bringing this book from dream to reality.

The project was set in motion through the affirmation of Les and Kay Clemens. They received me in their home and introduced me to groups in their church where some of the stories were shared verbally. To facilitate my task of filling in sketchy outlines and taking notes from diaries and interviews, they provided me with a home computer. It enabled me to work at Papa's bedside and capture his heartbeat. I will always treasure their practical assistance and continued friendship through the long tedious process.

I am grateful to my two brothers Bud and Mark who were behind the effort from the beginning. I thank them for relieving me from a heavy workload to complete this task. Bud's advice and help on the manuscript, particularly by adding details on events occurring before my birth or when I was too young to understand, was most helpful. Thank you, Bud and Mark, for all we've shared and learned through the experience.

I wish to thank my extended family for their encouragement, especially my twin aunts, Aunt Ruth and Aunt Esther, along with Uncles Ed Heinrichs and George George, as well as Aunt Jeanette, who cheered me on. I seem to hear Aunt Esther chuckling in Heaven with Aunt Kathryn over the completed project. I'm grateful to Aunt Emma and Uncle Willard for sharing their home with me for three months, allowing me to pick up the abandoned manuscript, as well as Uncle Art, Uncle John, and Aunt Eva for many tokens of kindness.

Many are those who read and critiqued the manuscript from the first draft on. Cousin Dusty offered valuable insights as I saw pages through her eyes. David Kopp gave an honest critique on the first draft, as well as Irvin and Lydia Friesen. My heartfelt thanks goes to Warren Wiersbe for giving liberally of his time to read and endorse the manuscript and to Fred Bloomer for helping with the last proofreading. I also thank God for my African "aunts" and "uncles" who had a profound impact on my life and cheered me through this book. Among just a few are: Anna Enns, Kathryn and Martha Willems, John and Ruth Kliewer, Elsie Guenther, Anna Goertzen, Tillie Wall, Elsie Fischer, Clyde and Elizabeth Shannon, and Arnold and Rosella Prieb.

I am deeply grateful to all who played a part in my cultural adaptation to America, where the project was completed. My first angels were Joanne and Bob Heinmiller, Chris and Joan Ardovannis, Bob and Gloria Fenter, and Roy and Gerry Rigsbe. Craig and Jessi LaChance have, from the start, been my traveling angels. They provided and maintained my vehicle—as did Earl Bowans. Numerous are those who provided technical or practical assistance, or generous and warm hospitality. I thank all, and particularly these: John and Ellen Hash, Ray and Betty Miller, Steve and Peggy Floreck, Judy Sloper, Adriane Pendleton, Steve and Kathy Martens, Sharon and Johnny Quiring, Cliff and Shirley Neufeld, Ted and Alida Palmatier, Marshall and Marilyn Matthews, Ed and Lillian Vinson, Dr. Steve Davis, and Dr. Bill Lyons. I thank LaVerne Lyman for sharing her home, and Helen Margene too. She, along with Lorayne Smith, Rose Fadenrecht, and Anna Ediger, have shown themselves to be four wonderful "Moms." I'll always be grateful for the long-term friendship of Nick and Lydia Martens, Henry and Anne Hooge, and Luella Helms, who partnered through more than fifty years of my parent's careers, and plodded on with mine.

I'm deeply grateful to David and Cleo McMartin who—with God's approval—lured me to their quiet country cottage where I could think and write. More valuable than anything else has been their affirmation. It permitted me to cope with the emotional aspects involved in completing the manuscript. To the friends who make up the group that livens up my "hideout" twice a week, and who helped in untold ways while keeping me accountable, I acknowledge gratitude: Hattie Beal, Dorothy Mahoney, Sue and Jerry Webber, Paul and Kay Galea, Dan and Jackie Myers, Jill Johnson, Sandy Camri, Chris King, Walter and Georgenne Snook, Sheila MacGregor, the LeRoys, and Kate Santero.

I thank in a special way Ronda Santero and Patti Stucki for opening my eyes to the throbbing wounds of the street people and the unchurched in America. Patti is one of many who carries painful childhood memories. Ronda was my neighbor whom I knew casually—until the day the police burst into her home and arrested her husband Rick and herself for growing marijuana. From age 24 Ronda had professed belief in Christ, but a painful experience had shoved her out of the church. From that moment on she turned her back on God and went her own way. It wasn't until she was "busted" 16 years later that she fully realized how far she'd wandered. She was now ready to surrender—to the authorities and to God. Circled by the prayers of the Bible study group who stood with her through the ordeal, attending court hearings and affirming confidence, she began to take steps in the right direction. Still, she needed to pay her dues to society. During the boring days of house arrest she read the manuscript and gave honest appraisal. It was her input that enabled me to orient the writing to include church orphans and street wanderers who are the pulse beat of her heart. The turnaround in the life of her husband Rick was equally dramatic; helped by one-on-one Bible study with "Pops," he has developed spiritual muscle and has been a true "brother" to me.

Thanks to all of you for being a part of this book.

Most of all I thank my Heavenly Father for providing "manna" each day and for blessing me through so many people and in so many ways throughout this project.

Dedicated to

all children—young and old—
who carry painful memories.
May this book sweeten the bitterness
and draw you close to your Heavenly Father
who loves you.

Contents

Chapter		Page
	Foreword	xi
	Preface	xv
	Introduction	xvii
1	Dusty Boots on Crooked Paths	1
2	Bare Feet Between Two Continents.	7
3	Baby Shoes With Immigration Tags	13
4	Muddy Shoes on Polished Floors	15
5	Skating Shoes on Bending Ice.	19
6	Smelly Shoes in a Moving Hog Pen	21
7	Child Shoes Surrounded by Giants	25
8	Sloppy Shoes in the Boot of a River Rat	29
9	Bright Shiny Shoes Polished by Grace	33
10	Stiff Shoes...on Firm Ground	37
11	Dainty White Pumps...Well, Not Quite.	41

Chapter   **Page**

12   Solid Shoes on Solid Rock   45

13   Hot Shoes...From a Flaming Touch   49

14   Strange Shoes in a Strange Land   57

15   Wooden Shoes on Rough Cobblestones   61

16   Belgian Carpet Slippers on Hardwood Floors . .   67

17   Sailing Shoes Facing New Horizons   71

18   Exploring Shoes on the Land of Dreams   77

19   Sooty Shoes Initiating Service   81

20   Braced Shoes to Prevent Falling.   87

21   River Shoes...on Uncrossable Waters   91

22   New Shoes Breaking Into a New Life   99

23   Reckless Shoes Plunging Ahead. 111

24   Floppy Shoes With Startling Strength 119

25   Elastic Shoes...Expanding With Trust 125

26   Pumped Up Shoes...With
        the Breath of the Spirit 133

27   Misplaced Shoes on a Detour 137

28   Artificial Shoes in Wonderland. 143

29   Safari Shoes—With God at the Wheel 151

30   Untied Shoes Prepared to Change 159

31   Walking Shoes With Treasured Moments. 165

32   Cozy Shoes in a Humble Home 169

33   Light Shoes...in a Dark Night 175

34   Heavy Shoes in Black and White 181

35   Bright Sandals in Colors of Faith 187

36   Garden Shoes Sowing and Reaping 191

Chapter		Page
37	Eager Shoes and Spinning Wheels	195
38	Army Boots on Crippled Feet	201
39	Ordinary Sandals Extending Grace	207
40	Tiny Shoes in God's Hands	213
41	Everyday Shoes on Sacred Ground	221
42	Disability Shoes Bouncing on a Sea of Love	225
43	Traveling Shoes With Journey Mercies	235
44	Following Shoes Behind the Man With the Pitcher.	243
45	Confident Shoes Trusting the Captain	249
46	Glossy Shoes Polished With Patience	255
47	Combat Boots on Decisive D Days	259
48	Changing Shoes Over Shifting Sands	263
49	Worn Shoes Homeward Bound	269

Foreword

Shoes have always fascinated me. The endless shapes, sizes, and colors seem to personify the people wearing them. They denote age, health, professions, events, styles, and tastes. I remember fondly the shoes of my past: the little red sandals that traveled thousands of miles and crossed many African rivers to reach me in time for my fifth Christmas; the stiff, sturdy shoes that "Papa" insisted were "good for me"—until he saw my blisters; my first long-wished-for pair of high heels...

Among all the other *shoes* in my life were, of course, those of my parents. Mama's were oversized and spoke of swollen, painful feet, but Papa's shoes held me spellbound. One observation I'd made was they were in constant need of repairs. Since there usually wasn't a shoe repairman in the vicinity, he'd fix them himself using scraps from tires or other recycled materials. Then there was his quaint enjoyment of the chore of keeping the family's shoes polished; his own usually received a few extra swishes of the brush just before he left the house. Though the shine hardly lasted more than a few steps beyond our door, that little performance seemed to pronounce his readiness to face the day. Later in the evening, after dinner, he'd sit down, unfasten his shoes and slip out of them. To me he appeared like a soldier taking off his armor. I would sometimes pick up those shoes and feel their warmth and strength as stories were told about where they'd walked that day. Much later, however, I discovered more profound lessons. One lesson was that those ordinary shoes illustrated Isaiah 52:7: "How beautiful on the mountains are the feet of those who bring good news, who proclaim peace...." Though Papa's shoes were ordinary and imperfect, they trekked dusty paths on many mountains—and countries—and his footprints proclaimed peace. How beautiful are all of our shoes when we're faithful where God puts us. Each shoe has its own sparkle and quaint characteristics.

When the sun began to set on Papa's life—through the discovery of a brain tumor—we decided it was time to describe the "stones of remembrance" or the *shoes* in his life. We got out Mama's diaries and began talking. It was during that time that I bought for Papa his last pair of shoes. These were Christmas slippers in red and green felt with gold trim. He was proud of those slippers and I was pleased to see them sitting beside his bed, a reminder of the European custom of putting out shoes—not stockings—for Christmas, and the symbolism of leaving them out for God to fill with blessings.

Much of this writing developed from Mama's diaries along with Papa's outlines and sketchy stories. Some of our critique sessions were animated as Papa considered details of personal hardship unnecessary. Readers were supposed to read between the lines or use their own imaginations. Usually I would comply with his wishes, but following his death I included some details that we'd discussed, which were never intended for publication. *Forgive me, Papa.* Other information was added after interviewing some of his contemporaries, coworkers, and family members as well as after the results of my own research. Time together ran out before we were able to finish it entirely. The rough draft on this first volume was completed before Papa's death. About one fourth of the second volume was written before Mama's sudden departure. A considerable period of time elapsed before was able to pick up and complete the project.

I hope you'll enjoy walking in the shoes described in this first volume and that your appetite will be whetted for the increased momentum of volume two. It's my prayer that you'll identify your own shoes in the following chapters and that, in putting them out for God's touch, you'll find them packed full of blessings.

Preface

"There is no end to the making of books," said Solomon. Recountings of life experiences continue to fill shelves the world over. The greatest and most worthy account ever written is recorded in God's Book in the life of His Son Jesus, who lived and walked on this earth for 33 brief years. His biographers, Matthew, Mark, Luke, and John, give many details. Still, John ends his account by saying, "Jesus did many other things as well. If every one of them were written down, I suppose that even the whole world would not have room for the books that would be written."

When considering the life of Jesus, one would hardly dare to write of anyone else. It's of Him that John the Baptist— "the greatest among men"—exclaimed, "His sandals I am unworthy to stoop down and untie" (see Mk. 1:7). It's my desire that He will be seen in the pages that follow. His ways and dealings with humanity are mysterious. Many are the lessons we learn too late.

Soon after my conversion a booklet by Keith Brooks, then editor of Biola's magazine, *The King's Business*, was given to me. The title of the booklet was *Things God Uses*. This was the brightest ray of hope since my discovery of grace. I thought my life had already burned out serving Satan, but what patience, wisdom, and power our Savior has. Often He works with the most unlikely materials to produce trophies. I have never ceased to marvel at the working of His grace in my life. If He can do it for me, He can do it for you. No matter what your past may be, your future shines as bright as His shining grace.

Abe Kroeker
Braine-le-Chateau, Belgium
January 1989

Introduction

Whenever or wherever God has a task to perform, He has a man to fit the task. In this case the man was Abraham F. Kroeker, or just plain "Abe" as we all called him. The task began in dusty villages of Africa and expanded to three continents, spanning many languages and cultures.

The title *Shiny Shoes on Dusty Paths* is more than an eye-catcher. Besides the many facets of life described in the pages that follow, I was impressed with the meticulous care Abe took in the details of his daily walk.

To illustrate his *Shiny Shoes*: after having lived in Africa three years, my wife Lydia and I wanted to purchase a pair of pinking shears that Abe had brought with him from America. In spite of the hassles of packing and traveling, Abe walked to his files and pulled out the original receipt.

In the *Dusty Paths* I see his humility and obedience to God. He never boasted about himself or his accomplishments. Remembering his life before his encounter with God, he'd marvel how—of all people—God could use him.

Abe was a man like Caleb, of whom it could be said that he wholly followed the Lord. Whatever he set his hand to do, he did thoroughly. He was equally dedicated in his relationships to God and man. He loved the Word of God, getting up early in the morning to study. He fully trusted the Lord and was willing to follow Him, even when he couldn't see the path ahead and where it led. Having strong convictions, he never compromised in areas of truth. His passion was to lead people into a personal relationship with Jesus Christ. Often he could be seen with his right hand in his hip pocket, his left foot forward, and his eyes fastened on those of the one to whom he was speaking, telling him or her of the love of Jesus and warning of the consequences of rejecting God.

He seemed bold and unafraid, but on one occasion he confided to me that each time he spoke to someone about the Lord, it was a real struggle. Yet he was faithful. Being a man of vision, he perceived that Christian literature could accomplish much more than the witness of a single individual—though not replace it. Even in Africa I was personally helped by books he had imported for missionaries. Later, of course, this vision for literature became the major focus of his ministry. He was a man of influence, providing leadership for Christian publishers and distributors throughout Europe.

This book is not only about Abe; it's about God. One sees God calling and preparing His man for specific work. Delays and difficulties en route to Africa—though not understood at the time—were used by God to direct His man to an expanded outreach. One sees God unlocking and opening doors that had seemed tightly closed, and then adding blessing. Since the task is God's, it continues when His servant is called "home."

The book is also about ministry. The Bible says that the gospel is "the power of God for the salvation of everyone who believes" (Rom. 1:16). Ministry is the spreading of this "good news" to every person. Naturally, this cannot be done by one person alone. God calls others to help in the endeavor, and He uses other means of communication, such as literature. Literature speaks many languages, can relate to many cultures, and talks to the heart. It travels cheaply and can speak, at the same time, to many people in many different places. Here is a story of how the gospel was proclaimed in Africa where an autonomous church now stands, and then expanded to Europe, French Canada, and various islands.

This book is about a family, for Abe didn't work alone. His family struggled beside him as he laid the foundation for mission stations and the literature work in Belgium. Today the family has extended to include many in Africa, Europe, and the American continent.

God's call for us may not lead in the same paths as Abe's, but each of us has a specific place and purpose. May this book challenge us anew to trust God completely and to follow where He leads.

Irvin L. Friesen
Coworker and friend

1

Dusty Boots on Crooked Paths

Speed, thrills, alcohol, and
my motorcycle gang—that was life.
Dallas, Oregon
1927

The speedometer on my motorcycle climbed steadily as I
sped down the open highway, passing every moving vehicle
on the road. The wind, the speed, the risk—that was life. If
only it could go on forever.

Regretfully I turned off the highway and entered the
sleepy little town of Dallas, Oregon. Stopping with a screech-
ing halt in front of a tavern, I dismounted and walked in.

Heads turned with expectancy, watching as my heavy
dusty boots clattered across the uneven boards of the tavern
floor. I slid onto a stool and pushed back my disheveled hair.

"Hi Abe, what's new?" greeted the bartender.

I watched him fill a foaming mug of beer and place it on the counter before replying. "Had another wreck last night," I stated matter-of-factly as I reached for my mug. After draining it with hardly more than a breath I added, "Flew six feet in the air and landed in the middle of the highway right on my car seat." I slid my mug across the counter for a refill.

"Wow," cheered my admirers. "What happened?"

None of the customers listening to the humorous rendering of my latest escapade could have imagined that below my cocky facade was an anguished soul. Exhilaration, thrills, fast buddies, and alcohol were supposed to relieve boredom and fill a nagging emptiness. Instead, they increased the vacuum and pointed a nagging finger at the crooked path my dusty boots were walking.

The night before, heedless of prohibition restrictions, my friends and I had been to a party in Portland where drinking provided the main recreation. Driving back, in a state of drunken stupor, we had difficulty following signs and signals. We barely recognized the fact that we were driving on railroad tracks. By some miracle we connected to the Portland-Salem road, but my foggy head was unable to keep the car on the right side of the road. Through the haze I saw headlights facing us that grew increasingly bright. Before we came to a complete stop three cars had collided. As I flew through the air a voice resounded in the back of my head, "This is your last chance, Abe." In a few brief seconds I saw my life displayed before my eyes. I saw Mother coming to the door to meet me at one or two in the morning, after one of my nights out. I knew by the look in her eyes that she'd been praying for me. I saw my sister Kathryn, who never spoke down to me even though she knew how low I'd fallen. I saw the concerned face of Mrs. Wilson, the mother of one of my buddies. Her heart had broken by her son's decadent life style, and she'd been praying that I, at least, would escape before falling so low.

When all the noise of the crash had subsided, I found myself still sitting on the car seat—but on the ground outside the car. I jumped up quickly as if to adjust my outward mask of tough nonchalance, but the cracks within were widening and bordering on desperation.

For several years I'd chased around with my motorcycle gang, mocking the religious "thou shalt nots" of my fanatic Mennonite family. No dancing, no movies, no games on Sunday, no fun, no nothing. That was not for me. Recklessly I plunged into the fast life, heedless of consequences.

I joined a lodge that met on a dance floor in town and made frequent visits to all the taverns where my repertoire of jokes, adventures, and nonsense gave me the reputation of prime entertainer and good customer.

One night after drinking a few too many glasses, my gang stood on the street outside the church mocking the singing inside. Someone must have tipped off the cops, for they soon appeared and arrested us before the pained eyes of my parents. After a night in jail, the emptiness I'd tried so desperately to fill was more hollow than ever.

Some time later the men's chorus from the Bible Institute of Los Angeles (Biola) came to the Dallas high school for a concert. I couldn't help but notice the serenity on the faces of the fellows as they sang and told how God was part of their lives. Nor could I repress an acute longing for the peace of which they spoke.

The final blow came when evangelist William Peach came to town for a week of meetings. He was then assistant pastor of the Church of the Open Door in Los Angeles. I sneaked into a few services, just to please Mother, though she was never aware of my presence. To my astonishment, the evangelist spoke on my wavelength.

The following Friday I was miles from town when I felt an irresistible urge to attend the service. Taking shortcuts on dusty country roads, I stepped hard on the accelerator, managing to arrive just as the meeting was starting. The place was full with standing room only. I don't recall the message or text. I just knew God was speaking to me through that preacher. When the invitation was given, I ran outside and cried like a child.

Finding me in this condition, a neighbor friend asked, "What's wrong, Abe?"

I didn't answer. There was plenty wrong.

He insisted we go back inside. I hesitated, but finally turned my dusty boots toward the door. As I walked in the evangelist was quoting John 6:37, "All that the Father giveth Me shall come to Me; and him that cometh to Me I will in no wise cast out" (KJV). Those words penetrated my soul. Was there still hope for someone as low as I? The walls of resistance were crumbling.

The attendance at these meetings was so large that the church became too small. So the dance floor, where my lodge met, was rented for the Sunday evening service. That night Evangelist Peach spoke on Revelation 3:20, "Behold, I stand at the door, and knock: if any man hear My voice, and open the door [of his heart and life], I will come in to him [live in him], and will sup with him [communicate intimately with him], and he with Me" (KJV).

When the invitation was given, I walked to the front and knelt on that floor. I was oblivious to who was there and what people thought. My heart's door had swung wide open. Overwhelmed that God would bother Himself with such as I, my heart now ached to give Him my all.

The sense of gratitude, relief, and joy continued in the days that followed. The emptiness that had driven me to wild pursuits was filled with God's immeasurable grace. For the rest of my life I've tried, unsuccessfully, to understand and express what that grace means to me. The closest I can come is through a sense of identification with John Newton, the hardened slave trader who penned the words of the song "Amazing Grace."

Amazing grace how sweet the sound,
That saved a wretch like me
I once was lost, but now am found,
Was blind, but now I see.
Twas grace that taught my heart to fear,
And grace my fears relieved;
How precious did that grace appear
The hour I first believed.

Having all my sins removed was like having my dusty boots polished to a shimmering glow. They were now ready to walk the dusty paths of life.

By this time news had already traveled to all the taverns and to my gang. The gossip of the week was, "Have you heard the latest? Abe's got religion."

"Abe! Imagine *him* falling off the deep end!"

"Yes, and get this, he's even talking about being a missionary. Can you imagine? Abe in Africa?"

"Yeah, I can imagine him chasing savages, but...what does he know that we don't?"

For me, the only shadow was regret over wasted time. Why had I resisted so long? Later I would realize that God had been tracking me all along. Each awkward footstep was known by Him: My childhood, my peculiar family, and my restless pursuits were preparing me for adventures beyond my wildest imagination. God's plan for each life is thrilling and follows a skillfully designed plan. Let me take you back to events just prior to my birth and the continent where it all began.

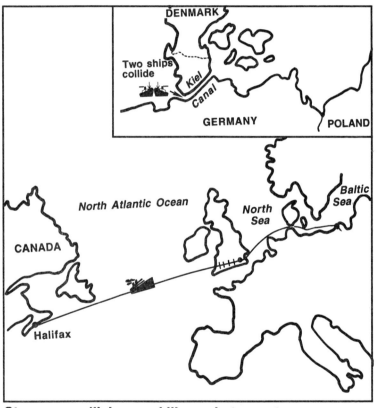

Storms, a collision, and illness between two continents

2

Bare Feet Between Two Continents

For three months the ship inched its way
against the storm.

Karkhov, Russia
1903

A touch of autumn in the early morning air had wrapped a white blanket around the sleeping town of Karkhov, Russia. A darkly clad family huddled against the central post office waiting the arrival of the post coach.

The sound of hoofbeats in the distance announced the approaching horses, and eventually a carriage pierced the fog as it slowed to a stop. The coachman grabbed some postal sacks and jumped down from his high perch. With a nod and a flip of his hat he acknowledged the waiting passengers before entering the post office. Soon he reappeared burdened with even heavier sacks, which he slung onto the back of the coach before opening the carriage door for the family.

First he helped the young mother, obviously pregnant, up the steps, then hiked up a little boy appearing to be about two and another about five years old. Once the father, with a one-year-old in his arms, had stepped in and sat down, the coachman closed the door and climbed onto the high seat. With a crack of the whip the horses picked up their burden and disappeared into the white cloud, leaving behind only the fading sound of hoofbeats on rough cobblestones.

Only a few had witnessed the family's quiet departure from Karkhov, Russia, on that morning of September 25, 1903.

The passengers, Peter and Katharina Kroeker with their children Peter junior, Jacob, and baby Kathryn, sat in quiet wonder. Never again would they see the country and life that had been home for only a couple of generations. Baby Kathryn—whom they nicknamed Tina—would never remember the land of her birth. Their grandparents, thinking to find a land where they could worship without fear of prison and persecution, had left the lowlands of Europe to travel northward to Russia.

Memories stirred as they passed familiar scenes. The land that had become dear to their hearts seemed to be calling after them, "Why are you leaving? Did we not provide abundantly for your families?"

Russia had indeed been a happy and comfortable refuge. Fertile fields stretching over many acres had provided vast estates with lush harvests for many Mennonite families, including themselves. Their hard work ethics and agricultural inventions had permitted them to rise above the status of their neighbors. Spacious homes and gardens kept immaculate by devoted servants provided gracious living.

For a time soft breezes had blown away the fears and cares of the past they'd known in the lowlands. But now dark clouds were gathering over the beautiful land they'd grown to love, predicting the soon coming of violent storms of oppression and suffering.

The Russian government, under Catharine the Great, had encouraged these hard-working Mennonites to inhabit the underdeveloped areas of Russia, promising monetary compensations, freedom of religion, and exemption from military service. Now their high standard of living was becoming cause for resentment.

Some Mennonites used their affluence to benefit their workmen and needy neighbors. Others overlooked the needs of the peasants around them and grew cold in the false security of materialism. Some mingled with the Russians, sharing with them the faith dear to their hearts. Others lived in sophisticated ethnic islands, holding to the Dutch and German languages and emphasizing religious traditions rather than following the example of Christ.

Katharina remembered how concerned her father had been about these inconsistencies. With a fluent knowledge of the Russian language along with a caring disposition, he'd had numerous opportunities to demonstrate his beliefs. His servants were considered as members of the family and when anyone approached him with a need, he'd stop whatever he was doing to talk and pray—even if it meant halting machinery and a crew of harvesters. Most of his converts were his employees.

Now all such activity was considered proselytizing and was punishable by imprisonment or confiscation of property. The last baptism had been performed in winter—the safest time of the year—by cutting a hole in a frozen pond while a relative, on horseback, kept watch for the feared guards.

The Bolsheviks, led by Lenin and Trotsky, had recently split from the Social Democratic Party. Drastic measures, which would affect further religious restrictions, were being rumored. Gangs were beginning to roam the countryside and were raiding, looting, and committing atrocities on Mennonite homes.

Peter and Katharina had agonized over the decision to flee Russia. It meant leaving behind their comfortable home, taking only the barest necessities. Saying "good-bye" to loved ones—both Mennonites and Russians, some of whom had come to faith in their home—was almost unbearable, but at stake was the future of their children. What greater gift could they give their descendants than freedom to worship the God of their fathers? Before such a treasure, the sacrifice of affluence and social standing seemed a small price.

Had they known all the risks involved in migrating with little ones, they might have hesitated. But Peter's eyes had been scrutinizing the dark clouds on the political horizon. He knew that freedom lay on the distant shores of America. It was now calling to them.

After boarding a steamship in Libau, Poland, they soon found themselves in the long narrow Kiev canal. The canal stirred memories in Peter's mind of the history books he'd used in teaching. They were leaving behind those fine schools he'd hoped his children would one day attend. But there was no time to reminisce now because baby Tina had fallen violently ill. With no available doctor and few medicines, the only recourse was prayer. Holding the child in his arms, the family knelt around him as he petitioned the God who'd brought them this far. Surely He wouldn't fail them now.

Suddenly a loud crashing sound pierced the air as the boat shook and finally shivered to a stop. Peter put little Tina into Katharina's arms before opening the cabin door. "What happened?" he asked some of the passengers who were running through the hall.

"Our ship has crashed," someone hollered back.

Peter joined the passengers climbing the metal stairs that smelled of paint and dead fish. As he stepped onto the deck his eyes took in a strange picture. Meshed together were two ships. Their *Anglo Davis* had collided with *The Johanson*, a sister ship, in the dark passage of the canal. As Peter wound through the crowds to view different angles, a crew member, dressed in a navy uniform, called out to the passengers, "Gather your belongings together and get ready to transfer to another ship."

Peter shoved his way to the stairs and joined the family. A glance at little Tina brought relief to his heart. The child was breathing normally. Gently he lifted the sleeping child from Katharina's arms, relieving her to reorganize their belongings.

Exhausting hours followed as passengers were jostled and herded to another ship. With relief Peter and Katharina settled their family into a crowded cabin. By hanging blankets around the bunks they provided a minimum of privacy and quiet for their weary children. As they sang their familiar German hymns, the children slipped into sleep and the ship entered the open sea.

Again the quiet was shattered, this time by a loud thunderbolt. Soon the ship began to rock and sway, creak and crack. With each passing moment the tossing became more violent. Katharina clung to the metal bars of the bunk to steady herself while Peter tried to maintain enough balance to reach the door. Fearing that the storm might become more intense, he wanted to make sure his family had an ample supply of drinking water. In this his worst fears were realized, for the following day the storm became so violent that the crew, fearing shipwreck, spoke of turning back. To their relief the winds and waves calmed down, giving them courage to continue the voyage. Alas, the reprieve was brief. Again the storm broke out in all its fury. Thus for three months, as the ship inched its way across the Atlantic, the passengers wrenched with seasickness. When the Kroekers at last caught a first glimpse of their promised land, Peter burst into song while Katharina rubbed her swollen stomach, as if to reassure the barefoot child who was impatiently kicking against his confined quarters that he'd be taking his first steps on free soil.

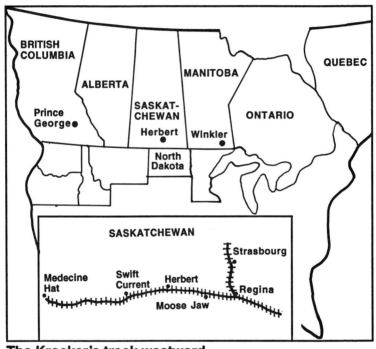

The Kroeker's treck westward

3

Baby Shoes With Immigration Tags

Abraham! A heavy name for a tiny baby.
Winkler, Manitoba
1904

A long train ride brought the weary family to Winkler, Manitoba, where Peter was offered a position as editor for a German newspaper. Katharina barely had time to put out a few treasured pictures as a finishing touch to the settling of her family into a modest home when, on February 19, 1904, she gave birth to her fourth child and third son, whom she named Abram. Later, however, as Peter was recording the birth, he suddenly decided to change the name to Abraham, Learning of this, Katharina questioned her husband. "What's wrong with Abram?" she asked.

"Nothing," responded Peter.

"Then why did you change it? Abraham is such a heavy name for a tiny baby."

"His name is Abraham," Peter insisted. "It's like Abraham of the Bible. We're not changing it again."

Though Katharina lost no time in shortening the "heavy" name to Abe, she wondered what impression the name would make on her son's footprints in the world.

Such matters were of no concern to me, the child adjusting to baby shoes with immigrant tags marked by struggles and sacrifices that as yet, I had no capacity to appreciate. So as the baby shoes were replaced by toddler and child-sized shoes, I'd be stumbling over my own headstrong nature and falling over obstacles of my own making.

Herbert, Saskatchewan
1906

When I was two the family moved to Herbert, Saskatchewan, where Father obtained a homestead. Here our family lived in a little sod house while Father built a permanent home and established a business of selling a variety of products, from household goods to farm implements, to toys and candy.

Mother took care of the homestead and gave birth to her fifth child, a little girl who was named Eva. Two years later little Mary was born, but she lived for just a few hours. Mother bore her sorrow bravely and quietly. The following year she was comforted by the birth of Emma, and was overjoyed four years later to receive another boy, whom she proudly named Sammy.

Our family of nine was now well-established in our new country, but remained separate from the rest of the community, retaining our European customs: our way of dressing, our foods, our family traditions, and especially our beliefs.

From attending school, we children adopted the English language while our parents clung to their mother tongue of German and Platz Deutsch (low German). Eventually they too would loosen their grip on these languages, but speaking several languages in the home permitted us young ones to be trilingual, an advantage that would later prove beneficial, particularly to me.

4

Muddy Shoes
on Polished Floors

They knew how to chew tobacco, aiming
their spit...a tremendous art.

Herbert, Saskatchewan
1910

As a boy I didn't particularly appreciate the name of
Abraham—not even the shortened version of Abe—though it
was somewhat better than *Douwe nichts* or *good-for-nothing*,
the nickname I was given a few years later by one of our
housemaids. I earned the title by walking with my muddy
shoes across her newly washed kitchen floor to grab an am-
monia cookie or to snitch a freshly baked bun called *zwie-
bach*. There's something about being tagged with such a
name. A child usually tries to live up to it—and this I did
very well.

Mother had plenty of chores, not only with her livestock of horses, cows, and pigs, and with sowing and harvesting the garden, but especially with the stock of her rapidly growing family. It was a relief for her when she could put me in school at the age of seven, though I looked younger, as I was rather small and pale.

As children, we all were like so many independent upstarts and war was not uncommon among us. One day Mother had just about had enough. Looking over our faces she exclaimed, "You're nothing but a bunch of no-count heathen."

"Come on, Mother," contested sister Eva, "we're not all that bad."

"Not one of you is an angel," shot back Mother.

"Were you, Mother?" asked Eva.

Silence was Mother's reply.

Father had a variety store on Main Street in Herbert where he sold literally everything from soap to peanuts. There was one item, though, on which he never made a profit: candy. This we passed out liberally to gain points with our friends. When we started playing marbles for keeps, the supply of that item also depleted rapidly in Father's store.

In spite of these leakages and the fact that he had a strong competitor just across the street, Father's business thrived. Soon he decided to build a larger store on a plot around the corner from his competitor. This enabled him to include clothing in his line of merchandise. The town hall was our neighbor on one side and the main hotel, with a bar on the ground floor, was our neighbor on the other. This position provided us with front row seats to most of the town's activities.

Father's competitor was a Jewish man by the name of Brownstone. An excellent businessman, he provided for his family an affluent living and elegant home, complete with maids and servants.

Since the Jewish faith prevented Mr. Brownstone from working on the Sabbath, I was often called on to light the kerosene lights in their store on Saturdays. His son Joe soon became one of my close friends. We passed our time watching people come and go to the hotel or gawked with admiration at the men in the bar. They knew how to chew tobacco, aiming their spit at a brass spittoon halfway across the room and never missing. This Joe and I considered a tremendous art, one which we decided to develop ourselves.

Father never sold liquor or tobacco, but Joe's father did, so we were able to obtain a large plug of the stuff with no problem. However, with the growing suspicion in my family as to what was in our pockets, we soon had to do our practicing under a loose board of the wooden sidewalk. Similar habits followed before I ever entered my teens.

My association with Joe was of great concern to my parents and every means was used to separate us or to keep me out of mischief. In the spring they sent me 14 miles out of town to work on my Uncle Pete Nickel's farm. This involved holding the reins of five to six horses and walking all day behind a harrow, row after row, mile after mile, across the endless prairies. Although I loved horses, I soon tired of this. Uncle's horses weren't spirited. They were old horses purchased from an auction and Uncle didn't feed them well. Neither did he pay me for my work.

In summer, the family saw to it that I helped harvest the fields. During haying time, once the wagon was loaded and ready to move, Mother would order me to the top of the haystack. No doubt it was easier for her to keep an eye on me perched up there. However, with all the gopher holes it was also a precarious position. So it wasn't surprising that I took a tumble one day when the cart took a dip. Within seconds Mother was beside me. She picked me up and turned me round and round. When I got over my dizziness I found that I was no worse for the wear. Call it an old wives' remedy if you will, but in my case it worked like a charm.

5

Skating Shoes on Bending Ice

Ignoring my Bible, I picked up my skates.
Herbert, Saskatchewan
1914

In spite of all my shenanigans, I rarely missed Sunday School. I admired my teacher, Mr. Brandt, mainly for his patience as I so often disturbed the class. These outward shenanigans, however, were innocent compared to the wickedness that stirred within my heart. Had Mr. Brandt any idea of all that was going on, he probably would have dealt very severely with me.

We attended the Mennonite Brethren Church on Main Street. All the services and classes were conducted in our ethnic language of German. The Bible and hymnals were also in this language. The generation of our parents persistently spoke German while the teenagers felt they'd outgrown this language. We frequently voiced our opinions about the Church. "Why criticize people around us who don't go to church when we can't even invite them to come to ours where the services are in a foreign language?" we argued. Another European custom that clashed with the culture around us was the women sitting on one side of the church and the men on the other. "Why do we have to be peculiar?" we asked.

My grandfather, Jake Martens, who'd recently immigrated from Russia, was one of the three so-called *lay leaders* in the church. Some of the phrases repeated left me cold. We were admonished to "repent" and to "produce good works." I dismissed those clichés from my thoughts. They held no appeal to my pleasure-oriented mind.

Saskatchewan was a wonderful place for the winter sports of ice skating, tobogganing, and ice hockey. Skating was my favorite, either alone or arm in arm with a pretty girl. One Sunday, on a beautiful spring morning, I decided to skip Sunday school. Ignoring my Bible, I picked up my skates and walked to the town mill pond. After a few exhilarating rounds I noticed that the ice was "bending," as we would say, or turning to rubber. Refusing to heed the warning, I determined to try one more round. Just as I reached the middle of the pond, the ice broke and I plunged into the frigid water. By breaking off pieces of ice with my numb hands, I was able to swim to the edge of the pond. When I finally lay exhausted on the bank, I resolved never again to miss my Sunday school class. Had I been wise, I might have considered and heeded the blaring warning signals of which this experience was a part. I'd need a few more repetitions on that score, though, to reinforce the lesson.

6

Smelly Shoes in a Moving Hog Pen

As the last hogs were being loaded,
we darted in.

Moose Jaw, Canada
1916

In summer we rode horses, caught gophers, and jumped on and off moving freight trains. Gophers were stalked on the prairies by "starring." This we accomplished simply by pouring water in their holes and drowning them out. We sold the tails to the town clerk for a penny a piece. Since it took considerable water to drown the gophers, and the water had to be carried long distances, we ran out of patience with this sport.

I didn't read extensively as a boy, but I came across a series of books called *The Tramp Books* that held my interest.

As a result, I acquired the ambition to become a train tramp. There was a brakeman in our town whom I admired greatly. He would wait till the train had picked up speed and then, at the last minute, gracefully jump onto the observation car while people on the station platform clapped. I tried to perform the same stunt one day on a fast-moving freight train, but didn't prove to be as graceful as the brakeman. After losing my hold I fell and barely missed having my foot cut off. I never told Mother about this experience.

One evening at the dinner table Dad jokingly asked my brother Jake and me if we would like to go to Moose Jaw.

Of course we would!

"You can go if you ride along with the pigs in the hog car," he said.

Since these were difficult times, Father's customers, most of whom were farmers, sometimes paid their overdue accounts in livestock, butter, grain, or whatever they had. Consequently, from time to time, livestock had to be delivered to Moose Jaw, where they were traded for currency. A carload of hogs was being prepared to be shipped that very evening.

Neither Jake nor I said a word, but we looked at each other and with our eyes we said, "It's a go." We didn't dare look at Father. We knew the tell-tale wrinkles around his eyes would clearly indicate that he was joking.

After dinner we put on our overalls and with a lantern in one hand and a heavy stick in the other, we headed for the stock corral. Arriving just as the last hogs were being loaded, we darted in with them.

The hogs, however, violently contested our rightful position as first class passengers of that car. One boar, in particular, was most displeased that I had claimed the corner he had chosen to occupy. I had to use my big stick to convince him of my authority.

It was chilly in the hog car as winter was beginning to set in. We were beginning to wonder if it was such a good idea to join the hogs on their ride to the city after all when the train, which had a coal-burning engine, made a water stop. A brakeman passed by and heard us talking. Raising his lantern he called out, "It's pretty cold in there, boys; you'd better come back to the caboose with me."

That was too good an invitation to refuse. He opened the door to the warm caboose heated with a big coal stove. There sat my father, reading the evening *Free Press* from Winnipeg. When he saw his sons walk in, he dropped his paper!

We rode the rest of the way to Moose Jaw in comfort. The country odor of our clothes and especially our cruddy, smelly shoes must have inspired Father, for immediately upon our arrival, he escorted us to a clothing store where he purchased a new outfit for each of us. He then took us to a hotel and asked for some heavy towels and saw to it that we got a good scrub from head to toe.

After a night's rest we were ready to discover the city. It was the first time we had seen paved streets and we were much impressed. Our stop at the fire department seemed far too short. Big dappled horses stood by the door, ready at the ring of the bell to come out and take their places at the front of a fire wagon.

Our next stop was the stockyard where father took care of his business, and then on to the butter and ice cream plant. This was where father shipped the cream and butter the farmers gave him as payment. We were delighted when an operator of the ice cream machine reached over and gave each of us a large wooden paddle topped with ice cream.

After this, we headed back to the hotel for a dinner fit for kings. The tables were covered with white linen tablecloths and napkins. We had a big dinner, beginning with soup and ending with pumpkin pie and coffee—all for 25 cents each. It was the first time we had tasted pumpkin pie, so we requested the waiter to give us the recipe, to which he agreed.

We rode home in style in a fine passenger train. Mother had quite a surprise when her two sons appeared with their father. "Where have you been?" she asked. "I've been frantic with worry!"

"Remember our dinner conversation the night before I left?" Father asked. "You might have known they'd take me up on that foolish proposal."

Mother scolded by shaking her head, but couldn't conceal the laughter in her eyes. Later that evening she heard the whole story, especially about the pumpkin pie. The recipe was put to good use and after that she made pumpkin pie every year for my birthday. It was a change from the buttermilk pie which had previously been her big hit.

As I think back to this experience now, I see an illustration of Colossians 1:12-14. After riding the hog car of this world's sin, we are "qualified...to share in the inheritance of the saints in the Kingdom of light. For He has rescued us from the dominion of darkness and brought us into the kingdom of the Son He loves, in whom we have redemption, the forgiveness of sins."

7

Child Shoes Surrounded by Giants

Her example taught me more...
than even a college education.
Herbert, Saskatchewan

As family members continued to come from Russia, some of them became our close neighbors. With an assortment of ages, characters, and cultural differences, we rubbed on each other from many sides. There were episodes of heated discussions, but some of these relatives had a profound influence on my early youth.

There was my *Tante* (Aunt) Mary, a deaconess in the church. Since she was unmarried she lived with my grandparents who, much to the joy of my parents, had also come to Canada. She kept busy visiting and helping people—"to serve the Lord," as she put it. Yet, she felt she could be more effective if she got Bible school training. So she enrolled at

Moody Bible Institute. Going away by herself to Chicago was in itself a brave thing for a young woman at that time, but for her it was particularly daring because she spoke hardly any English.

She left by coach train, carrying her belongings in a small suitcase. By evening she was tired and decided to ask the porter for a pillow. So when the porter, a black man, came by she leaned over, placed her hand on her cheek, and asked for a *kissen*—the German for *pillow*. The poor man was somewhat embarrassed, but the message finally got through to him and she got her pillow.

Tante Mary persevered and completed her studies at Moody, but had only a few years "to serve the Lord." She died at age 36. Her example taught me more than a library full of books or a college education.

I also had great admiration for *Tante* Anna, of whom it was said, "No one could argue with her." I had some valuable lessons to learn from her.

But of all the members of my extended family, it was *Grospa* (Russian for Grandpa) Jakob who influenced me the most. His name should have been Philip, which means "lover of horses," for he loved them and took much pride in them. He fed them so well that their backs were almost flat. I inherited my passion for horses from him. He talked to them in German, Platz Deutsch (low German), or Russian, and they would always respond. His training of them was with the utmost patience—as one would train a child.

If he should leave Dolly, his saddle horse, on the prairie with her reins down, she would stay put. She never budged a foot, not even when other horses approached. When *Grospa* had her hitched to a buggy and galloping at lightning speed, he would delight in demonstrating four wheel brakes—long before car manufacturers knew about such things. *Grospa* would just say an emphatic, "Ho," and although he hardly pulled the reins, we were nearly thrown against the buckboard. I gathered some profound lessons from that illustration of obedience. When *Grospa* came into the barn in the

morning, all the horses would raise their heads. They knew
their master's footsteps as well as they knew his voice.

He must have trained the horse Elie for his sister, *Tante*
Bergen. Although *Tante* lived in a barn-house, where the
cold winds blew through the cracks of her unfinished home,
I was always eager to go spend the night at her homestead,
for *Tante's* horse was also my pony. Elie was trained to put
her head down when I wanted to get off. The first time the
neighbors watched this performance, they threw up their
hands and screamed. But I slid easily over her mane and
landed on my feet.

As a lad, it always seemed to me that *Grospa* did everything thoroughly, whether farming, building, or preaching.
He was also a "lover of souls." A cousin told me that he'd
met a man from Russia who had exclaimed, "I'm here, in
church, because of your grandfather. He stopped his thresh-
ing machine in Russia every day to read the Bible to us."

When relatives came to town for their shopping, they'd
sometimes spend the night with *Oma* and *Grospa* or meet together for other occasions. Every evening before bedding
down for the night, and in the morning at the breakfast table, *Grospa* would always read the Bible and each one would
pray.

They must have read something about hell one evening.
That night I was sleeping in a small room in the *hevel benk*, or
planing bench, which had a sideboard used for carpentry.
Suddenly I awoke screaming. I'd been dreaming that I was
burning in hell. It may have been what inspired me, years
later, to write a tract entitled *No Hell?* Not all the Scriptures
I heard made such strong impressions on my mind as that,
but I realize that I was privileged in that the people who read
them, believed them.

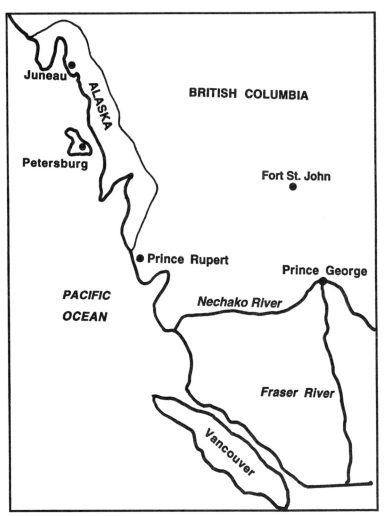

The tragedy of the Nechako River

8

Sloppy Shoes in the Boot of a River Rat

The tragedy should have
shaken me into serious thinking.
Prince George, British Columbia
1918

Father's ambitious spirit resulted in a thriving business with a combined grocery market and clothing store in Herbert and a branch store in Main Center. By this time World War I was waging full force, and there was a great demand for light spruce lumber to build tanks and airplane propellers. Father saw the possibility of another business venture. He decided to sell his two stores and move to British Columbia where timber was plentiful and where he could go into the logging and sawmill business.

So, once again, our family reluctantly pulled up roots. A long train ride brought us to the beautiful scenic town of

Prince George. Here Father set up his business and became an agent for the Grand Trunk Railway. This enabled him to assist the many people, still migrating from Russia, to locate homesteads. It was good land, but it had to be cleared of trees. They would have liked to clear it of the pesky mosquitoes as well, but they never succeeded.

Within a few years the number of children in our family grew from seven to ten with the arrival of Arthur, and the following year with twins Esther and Ruth. How well I remember the birth of my twin sisters.

Since we had no phone I was told to go to the house next door to call for the doctor. Feeling timid as I approached the house of the neighbor, and not realizing the importance of my errand, I knocked softly at their door. It was quite some time before I got a response, but when faces finally appeared at the screen door—and I had made my request—there was immediate action. "Why didn't you bang on the door?" they yelled as they ran to the phone.

In spite of the delay, the doctor arrived on time and everything went well. My sisters were strong and healthy and, to everyone else but me, they were identical. Even Mother had to tie different colored wool thread around their wrists, or a ribbon in their hair, to identify them. Later on they could play jokes on family and friends, but they never fooled me. For many things I lacked sense, but when it came to my little twin sisters, I had a sixth sense.

My brother Pete, who had been a schoolteacher in Saskatchewan from the age of 16, now obtained employment in the telegraph office of the Grand Trunk Railway. I too was able to get a job there as messenger boy, delivering telegrams. I later gave that up in order to start high school.

I wasted no time getting into mischief of all kinds. Throwing snowballs into school windows was a tame beginning. When I began to spend a lot of after-school hours in the pool halls, the family decided to put me to work in father's mill, which was located fifty miles north of town. I became a log driver or "river rat" bringing logs out of the

Fraser River into the sawmill. It was a dangerous job, but I was afraid of nothing. I had great respect for the loggers who felled the trees; they were rough and fearless men, as their occupation demanded. However, like many of them, I left the light of truth modeled before me by great people, and settled into the dark sloppy atmosphere of my soggy boots.

Once the logs were felled they were chained together and floated down river. We noticed that we were losing a lot of logs because of faulty links in the chains, so a used motor boat was purchased to pull the logs.

One Sunday afternoon 20-year-old Pete decided to take 11-year-old Eva and 4-year-old Sammy out on the Nechako River for a ride. When they got to the middle of the river, the motor stalled. The swift current caught the boat and smashed it against the pier. At that point Pete helped Eva get a footing on the pier. He then swam after Sammy. This time Pete's efforts were unsuccessful. The swift current—and perhaps a whirlpool—drew both boys under the surface. Indians on the bank, who saw what was happening, pushed their dugout canoe into the water and rushed to the two struggling brothers. Before they could reach them, the boys disappeared, never to come up again. Although the Indians searched for miles up and down the banks of the Nechako and Fraser Rivers, the bodies were never found.

This tragedy, which took place on June 23, 1918, should have caused me to do some serious thinking about my own eternal destiny, but my heart was hard.

Mother was deeply distressed. She went to an empty log house near our house and poured out the cries of her soul to God. Had it not been for the six-month-old twins, who required her care and whose sweet ways soothed her broken heart, she claimed she would have lost her mind.

Now Mother could no longer bear to live near that river, so the family disposed of everything and moved to the United States. Mother had a sister living on a farm near Dallas, Oregon, so we moved to that town. Here I would make the most significant decision of my life.

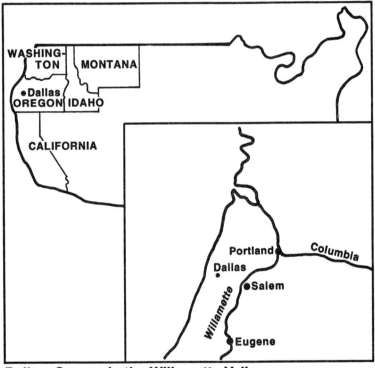

Dallas, Oregon in the Willamette Valley

9

Bright Shiny Shoes
Polished by Grace

I turned around and
left my old life behind.

Dallas, Oregon
1927

As the family was settling in Dallas, the Depression was crippling businesses the world over. It was not surprising that father's new business, growing and selling prunes, was not as successful as he'd hoped. Since he wasn't one to give up, he soon started another business selling pianos and sewing machines. I became his associate as salesman and service-man for the sewing machines. On the side, I also sold metal rat traps to hardware stores. I learned all the sales gimmicks, including, "Why mice and rats *prefer* steel to wooden traps." With time I developed quite a convincing sales pitch, so much so that one of my victims commented, as he reluctantly pulled cash out of his pocket, "Good grief, Abe, you could sell glasses to a blind Jew."

I attended Dallas high school during the time Father had the prune business going. My younger sisters, Eva and Emma, attended a little country school called Smithfield. From time to time they'd bring home a friend whose name was Mary, but I never paid much attention to her and she certainly didn't admire my life style or my gang. I'd become quite careless about my conduct.

Then that wonderful transformation happened that turned my life around. So overwhelmed by the immensity of grace and so filled with relief and gratitude, my previous life repulsed me. I turned around and left my old life behind. It was as if I'd exchanged my old dusty boots for a pair of bright new shiny shoes.

Soon the talk of the town, of the stores, the taverns, and the hangouts for young people, was "Abe Kroeker's religion." It wasn't "religion" that made the difference, but an extraordinary relationship. God, who had previously been far away, had come close. I could know Him and live for Him. This became a consuming passion. I no longer needed tobacco, liquor, the acceptance of my peers, or the thrills that carried heavy price tags.

The summer after my conversion a unique baptism took place in the LaCreole River. I was part of a group that included 30 people who had accepted Christ during the special meetings with Evangelist Peach.

Overwhelmed with the earthshaking changes in my life, I was bursting with excitement. Surprisingly some of the group seemed to be taking the step very much in their stride. *How could they remain so calm*, I wondered. I wanted to shout and scream.

Prior to the baptism, a special meeting was held during which candidates for baptism gave their testimonies. It was the first time I had publicly told about my conversion. On our way home after that meeting, my sister Kathryn said,

"Abe, you're going to be a preacher someday." I was stunned, but certainly not convinced.

I had expected the joy and excitement to cool off with each day, but for me, the more I realized the immensity of God's love and grace, the more thrilled I became. Soon a deep longing stirred my heart. I wanted more than just enjoyment of God. *Could I dare to offer myself to serve Him?* I wondered. *Could He find use for one who had wasted his life in sin and foolishness? Would he allow me such honor?*

I finally recognized that if God could extend grace to save someone like me, He could give grace for someone like me to serve Him. I offered Him my life and recklessly told Him I'd even be willing to be a missionary—if He'd have me.

Once that commitment was made, training became the most obvious necessity. For a missionary career such training would, of course, be an essential requirement. If I should never get to the mission field, there were still plenty of rough edges in my life that could use some chiseling and sanding. I was anxious to get on with it.

10

Stiff Shoes...on Firm Ground

My mind was made up.
Los Angeles, California
1929

Father was quite upset when I told him I'd decided to go to Bible school. The business was doing well; the future looked promising—even prosperous. My leaving would require many adjustments for him. He had wept with joy when I'd come to faith in Christ, but he wasn't prepared to lose his business partner.

For me the decision was part of my conversion package. Everything had changed—including the orientation of my life's work. Money, status, pleasure, and comfort had fallen from their lofty position as important goals for my future. "I've wasted enough time on insignificant pursuits," I argued. "I want to invest the rest of my life for God. You've just got to understand, Father. My mind's made up."

"Well, then, don't count on me for a single penny," was his final statement.

The words burned deeply. Time would change his heart and I would come to understand his shattered dreams. But the first lesson I needed to learn was that following in God's footprints sometimes requires standing in firm, stiff shoes. I packed my bags and, in the fall of 1927, found myself on a bus bound for the Bible Institute of Los Angeles, or Biola. A couple of weeks later I sat in a classroom where, for the first time in my life, I was anxious to learn.

Immature as I was, I struggled to understand some of the basic doctrines that Dr. McLain presented in an academic manner.

Also, since it was the Depression, finances were stretched to the limit and jobs were hard to find. I had to resort to janitor work and serving in sandwich shops, neither of which was satisfactory because I wasn't gifted in housekeeping skills and the pay was meager.

I decided to drop out of school for a semester to catch up on the debts I was accumulating. I went to Alberta, Canada, to help in the harvest with my Uncle Henry and then worked for a time in Father's business. Later a woman in an employment bureau discovered that I was quite a capable gardener. She took an interest in me and sent me to her home. Satisfied with my work, she found many jobs for me, including one as a gardener for the famous movie producer, Cecil B. Demille. I enjoyed tailoring his yard to a meticulous perfection and winding up by polishing the plants till they glistened in sunshine and shadow.

When I returned to school, I realized that many changes had taken place. Dr. McLain had accepted an invitation to become president of Faith Seminary in Winona Lake, Indiana, and Dr. John C. Page, previously from Moody Bible Institute, had joined the faculty of Biola as the new doctrine professor.

Dr. Page's style of teaching was primarily through dictation. As I took notes of the truths he was expounding, new insights opened to my soul. Once and for all I became established on essential issues, such as law and grace. Those notes, along with those taken from Keith L. Brooks and G. Campbell Morgan, I carefully typed after class. They later became one of my most treasured and useful possessions and were translated into Chokwe and Kikongo (African dialects).

Biola had a strong emphasis on personal evangelism—communicating to others how Christ can be known in a personal way—and we were frequently given opportunities to put our theory into practice. Shop teams were organized where, after a last drilling session, we went to restaurants and shops to give a short message or testimony and leave tracts. Sometimes we'd stay longer to talk with those who were particularly interested. This was called soul-winning. Though fearless on a motorcycle and an easy talker, I found the assignment a scary adventure. Bringing others to understand God's immense love and grace is one of life's greatest challenges. I learned that explaining spiritual truth requires spiritual power. Calling on that power and relying on it is the key. Another important element in soul-winning is drawing on the power of God's Book.

"Daddy Horton" (Dr. John Horton), the professor responsible for the personal evangelism program, taught by example. It was said that he never lost an opportunity to witness. For example, if he'd step on the toes of someone on an elevator he'd say, "Excuse me, sir, are you a Christian?" He later prepared a special edition of the Gospel of John with the verses pertaining to salvation underlined. This booklet, which has had a wide circulation, has been helpful to soul-winners and seekers alike.

Missions also played an important role at Biola. We had many good missionary speakers, including the son of Hudson Taylor, Rolland C. Bingham of the Sudan Interior Mission, and Charles Hurlburt with the Africa Inland Mission. I'd strain all my senses as I latched onto their words.

Mr. Farmer, of the South African Mission, came at a time when some of the students were rather rambunctious. Considerable energy was being spent on such pranks as hanging an effigy of a well-known character (usually a professor), in the gangway leading to the main lecture hall, or dropping bags of water from the roof of the 13-story building onto the sidewalk below. At one time Irwin Moon, who later became director of Moody Institute of Science, hung by his toes from a flagpole of that same roof in full view of all!

Before beginning his message that morning, Mr. Farmer said, "I see we have a lot of missionary potential here."

There was.

A mission conference took place a short time after that in the large auditorium of the Church of the Open Door. At the end of the conference I walked to the platform to respond to God's call for overseas missionary service. Beside me a young woman was making the same commitment. Her name was Mary Rose Neufeld. She was my fiancée.

11

Dainty White Pumps...Well, Not Quite

She dressed with style, but her shoes...
Los Angeles, California
1930

It had been a hot summer day in the middle of July, 1928, when the church organized a picnic. The potluck dinner had been delicious, with the usual variety of Mennonite specialties—seven sweets and seven sours. Everyone was relaxing on the grass and enjoying the refreshing breeze after the heat of the day. As I looked over the crowd of picnickers, I noticed the three Neufeld sisters, Elizabeth, Mary, and Anna, sitting together on the grass. One of the three caused my heart to beat wildly.

I had just completed my first year at Biola and was working for Father, trying to catch up on my finances. During that year at Biola I'd heard many missionary speakers, and had been particularly sensitive to the pleas for Africa.

For some time I'd been praying for a companion, but knew that my prospective bride would have to be prepared for the possibility of following me to Africa. My heart beat rapidly as I walked toward the three sisters. When I caught Mary's eye, I motioned for her to come. She stood up and walked toward me. I led her beyond the crowd of picnickers to a quiet place where we sat down on the grass.

The question I asked caused her mouth to drop open in surprise: "What would you think of being a missionary to Africa?"

Her immediate reply was, "I'm not ready to become serious."

During the course of the summer we saw each other from time to time. She was working in the home of a lawyer, keeping house and caring for the children. This kept us from having romantic dates, but when I went to the country to make calls for my work, I'd drop by and pick her up. Sometimes we'd take along the children of the lawyer.

I noticed that her feelings toward me were beginning to change. Others around me noticed that I was beginning to change too!

One evening my sister Kathryn's boyfriend, Art Bestvater, dared me to say to Mary "I love you" in low German. The phrase *Ich hav du gute* sounded real funny. I decided to take him up on his dare. So the next time I saw her, I leaned over and said, "*Ich hav du gute,*" and kissed her. I knew by her response that she was very serious.

The days that followed were filled with change. I gave her the application papers for Biola and she began making arrangements for going to Los Angeles, which for her, a shy country girl, seemed like the other side of the world.

Biola had strict rules about engagement. You were not allowed to become engaged the first year. So we never openly allowed ourselves to talk about marriage, but we had a mutual understanding.

The following summer I stayed in Los Angeles to work for Cecil B. Demille as his gardener while Mary went back to Oregon. I was able to purchase an engagement ring, which I then sent to her in the mail. I would have preferred slipping it on her finger myself, but I wanted her to have the joy of wearing it right away.

One thing I'd learned about Mary in our courting days was her embarrassment over her long, size ten feet. She dressed with taste and style, as much as her budget could afford, but could do little to disguise her "big boats." I saw her feet as long and slender, just like her fingers, one of which carried my ring. It was her eyes, however, that charmed me most of all. I could read into them what her words couldn't express.

On June 21, 1930, three days after Mary's graduation from Biola, we were married in the Wee Kirk of the Heather, a small chapel with a beautiful indoor flower garden along one side, with cages of birds among the flowers. This storybook chapel built into the hill with Scottish heather planted on the slopes, is a duplicate of the one in which Annie Laurie worshiped in Scotland. The history of Annie Laurie's life is the history of Scotland of her day. Her deathless love song, which has endured three centuries, continues to flicker in the hearts of romantic lovers, including mine:

> "Her body is like the snow drift,
> Her throat is like the swan
> And her face it is the fairest
> That e'er the sun shone on.

> "Her dew on th' gowan lying
> Is the fa' o' her fairyfeet;
> And like winds in summer sighing,
> Her voice is low and sweet.

"Her voice is low an sweet,
And she's a' the world to me;
Anf for bonnie Annie Laurie
I'd lay me down and die."

Because Mary's father had died when she was a child, she walked down the aisle on the arm of her sister Anna's new husband, Corny. She looked beautiful in her street-length dress and dainty white pumps. The canaries in the cages sang to the accompaniment of the organ, which my sister Eva played. Four girls from Biola's Glee Club sang a wedding prayer, and my sister Emma sang "I Promise You." Our attendants were classmates Clyde Landrum and Ruby Larsen, who themselves were later married.

It seemed like a dream when Mary and I stood at the altar to take our vows. When the minister asked the bride, "Do you take this man to be your lawfully wedded husband?" there was an emotional delay that continued almost too long. So I confidently spoke out: "We do." There was a ripple in the audience while the birds kept singing.

The pastor officiating was Harry MacArthur. He and I had developed a bond of friendship as we worked together in Kiwana, a boy's club. Being a young pastor, it was his first wedding. Later when Mary and I were in his church, he told us that he had been as nervous as the bride and groom.

After the wedding we had a lovely dinner at the Rosslyn Hotel with the family from Oregon. This would have been considered tame in comparison to some of the elaborate receptions of today, but we were extremely happy and thankful that the Lord had brought us together. Mary would prove, in the days to come, to be the perfect missionary companion for me.

12

Solid Shoes
on Solid Rock

An enormous rock
towered over the little town.
Los Angeles, California
1931

We established our new home in Eagle Rock, a little sub-
urb of Los Angeles. It was named after an enormous rock
that towered above the little town. In the afternoons the
shadow of the rock covered Wyota Street where we lived,
giving us the shade we needed that first hot summer.

We liked the symbolism we saw in that rock that, to us,
depicted Christ, our rock, fortress, defense, and protector. It
also seemed to affirm enduring hope for our marriage. We
knew we'd be facing the storms and struggles that all couples
have, but our marriage and our faith stood on a solid Rock,
one which would stand the test of time.

Our tiny house was located on a driveway behind a larger house. It had only three rooms and a bathroom, plus a screened porch in front and back. The front porch had a swinging bench and a large arbor of tiny fragrant roses, which were Mary's delight. The back porch served as a breakfast room. There was just enough room for a table, chairs, and an icebox.

At the time of our wedding, I was working for Community Industries, picking up castoffs that people were giving away. About one month after we were married I was walking between two houses when I tripped over a wire that I hadn't noticed. I knew immediately that I'd broken my arm. There was no other way to get to the compensation infirmary, about 30 miles away, than to drive myself. The next day my sister Kathryn with her husband Art and two year-old Marjie arrived with Mom and Dad Kroeker. My incapacity to work gave us time to relax together, which included a trip to Mexico.

After the summer we moved to another little house nearer to Biola on Alverado Street. It was located near a park not far from Aimee McPherson's temple. At that time she was in her glory and drawing large crowds. We attended just once out of curiosity, and saw Aimee walk in with a magnificent bouquet of red roses while the crowd cheered. We left with uneasy hearts. The worship of a creature—instead of the Creator—was too painful to watch.

Our new home was larger with two bedrooms and another big room over the garage. A friend and former student of Biola, Dave Quiring, rented that room and boarded with us. This helped boost our meager income. Mary enjoyed puttering in the garden and watching it burst into bloom. She planted cuttings of ice plant on the hillside that ended beside our driveway, and nurtured enormous geraniums that reached the roof.

For me it was back to school again at Sixth and Hope Streets in the heart of Los Angeles. Although it took some buckling down at first, I was soon lost in the truths of God's Word, enabling me to become more and more established and settled in my convictions.

That year was an eventful one at Biola. A crisis arose that led to the resignation of the president, Dr. McInnis. It began with his writing a controversial book, *Peter, the Fisherman Philosopher.* There were accusations from both sides and cliques developed among the students. Before the dust settled, some of the controversy spilled into the Christian press, with damaging results.

At the same time there were men like John Hunter on the faculty. They stood steady and "balanced the ship" till the storm passed. Before long, business went on as usual. As Edgar Alan Poe stated in one of his essays, "The barber kept right on shaving." This experience was instructive for us as students. We learned volumes from the example of the faculty, and we learned to be on guard against divisive factors that could pop out even in havens of truth like our Alma Mater.

We shared many good times of fellowship that year with fellow students, who have remained friends for life. Time flew by so fast that I was almost sorry when graduation came. The commencement exercises of that class of 1931 remain some of my best memories. The audience sang the song by James McGraham: *Go Ye Into All the World and Preach the Gospel.* The words sent chills up our spines because Mary and I had chosen that theme as our primary goal—for the rest of our lives.

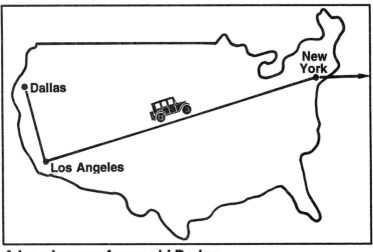

A long journey for an old Dodge

13

Hot Shoes...From a Flaming Touch

A sense of unworthiness
had turned my heart to ice.

Los Angeles, California
1931

As Mary and I started packing in preparation for leaving Los Angeles, our thoughts lingered on the experiences of the past few years, experiences that had changed the course of our lives.

The critical time for me had taken place when I was engaged to Mary and occupying a room in the school building. With every missionary speaker we heard, we'd wondered, *Is that where God wants us?*

Aaron and Ernestina Janzen had spoken in my home church in Dallas where they were told about my conversion and interest in missions. Consequently, Aaron made a special trip to Los Angeles to see me. After climbing to the sixth floor, he knocked on my door.

My answer, "Come in," was the opening of a door to Africa, although at the time I didn't recognize it as such. Aaron walked into my room and after seating himself opposite me, talked about Africa. I watched his expressions as he told about a large area of people who had never had an opportunity to hear about God's love for them. "We need your help," he said. "Won't you come to Congo, the center of Africa?"

I told him I'd consider it and pray about it. The next time Mary and I were together I told her about this visit. "It sounds like this might be the place for us," she said.

"It's just a small mission," I reminded her, "and it's in the interior of Africa where things are primitive and rough."

To my surprise, this didn't seem to be a problem for her. I was the one with cold feet.

I decided to go to the bell room on the roof of the thirteenth story to think and to pray. I grabbed my Bible and climbed the stairs. For a while I stood on the roof looking down at the street below where pedestrians and vehicles all seemed to be following some predetermined path. I wondered what God thought as He looked down on His creatures below. Some were following the way *He* had selected for them; no doubt others were going their own way. *What could be the right way for me?* I wondered.

I turned around and entered the bell tower. The bells had been taken out and the space transformed into a prayer tower. I knelt down and asked God to speak clearly. Then I opened my Bible and started paging through Isaiah, one of my favorite books. My eyes were drawn to chapter 6, titled *Isaiah's Vision.* It read: "...I saw the Lord seated on a throne, high and exalted.... Above Him were seraphs...calling to one another: 'Holy, holy, holy is the Lord Almighty....' "

Then came the dreadful words, "Woe to me!...For I am a man of unclean lips...."

The description fit me perfectly. Mockery from my own lips echoed through my mind with searing accusation. *You're disqualified*, it seemed to insinuate. Now I understood that an increasing sense of unworthiness had turned my heart to ice and was numbing my feet. I read on:

Then one of the seraphs flew to me with a live coal in his hand, which he had taken with tongs from the altar. With it he touched my mouth and said, "See, this has touched your lips; your guilt is taken away and your sins atoned for."..."Go and tell this people..." (Isaiah 6:6,9).

The words spoke with such intense clarity that I felt I was kneeling on holy ground. Earnestly I implored the touch of the fiery coal from the holy altar that would remove the nagging guilt. As I waited, the word *Go* came to the forefront of my mind. This was it for me. With astonishment and wonder I thanked God for that clear affirmation. When I got up I was so thrilled I wanted to scream my joy and relief from the rooftop. It was a moment I'll never forget.

For Mary, the matter was simple. "Your call is mine," she said. "When I agreed to marry you, I knew it would include this."

We could now make plans to move ahead. Our feet were shod with "the readiness that comes from the gospel of peace" (Eph. 6:15). We were anxious to run with it.

At that time, becoming a missionary was uncomplicated. Mission organizations didn't camp at Bible schools with an abundance of publicity, eager to give out application forms. We didn't apply to a mission. We simply informed the Janzens that the Lord had confirmed in our hearts that we were to serve with them.

Later Ralph and Edith Norton came to Biola and, during a chapel service, told of their work in Belgium. Mary and I were fascinated and even began wavering. "I wonder if we've made the right choice of destination," I told Mary.

"But we're already committed to Africa," Mary said, though she too was moved.

Finally we settled the issue, agreeing on a conclusive alternative: "If someday the door to Africa closes, we'll go to Belgium."

With the decision finalized, we prepared to go to Oregon to spend some time with the family and to visit some churches. Things fell in line, beginning with the purchase of an old Dodge that was almost as high as it was long. It was paid in full by my cousin Frank Martens, who later served many years with the British and Foreign Bible Society in British Columbia.

How precious and spiritually profitable were those few months with relatives and churches! We traveled over a wide area on the West Coast and in a few provinces of Canada. Meeting in small gatherings, usually in homes but sometimes in haylofts and even machine shops, we simply told what the Lord had done for us and our desire to serve Him in Africa.

We weren't eloquent, yet some who heard our testimony came to realize their own need to be delivered from the slavery of sin. I noticed particular interest on the part of farmers in the town of Winnipeg who had come to the city to do their shopping. As I gave my testimony at a street meeting, conducted by the Salvation Army, many stopped to listen.

Others were interested in our plans and offered to pray for us. Some would remain faithful for 50 years or more and in spite of thousands of miles that would come between us.

As the poet Tennyson wrote:

> I shot an arrow in the sky,
> It fell to earth, I knew not where
> I breathed a song into the air.
> It echoed again I know not where.
> For who has sight so keen and strong,
> That it can follow flight of song.
> Long afterward in an oak

I found the arrow still unbroken
And the song, from beginning to end
I found again in the heart of a friend.

Encouragement came through many kind words along the way as people opened their hearts. There were those, however, who stood and shook their heads. "You're going out on faith?" they'd ask. "You can't eat faith. Don't you think it's time to settle down and get a responsible job? Haven't you noticed that we're in a Depression?"

We admitted that our plans were vague and scary, and that we didn't have unusual faith. In fact, at times it seemed that others were exerting more faith than we ourselves.

Because of the Depression, people struggled to keep food on tables. Those who shared did so sacrificially. One farmer invited us to his home for the night after an evening meeting. I thought we'd never get going the next day, as there was such tremendous hospitality. This bearded man and his good wife had a number of orphans in addition to their own children.

Walking outside in the morning sunshine, this brother asked, "Do you need gas?" The old four-cylinder Dodge wasn't greedy on gas, but it needed more than faith to keep it running—in fact, it was empty that morning. After taking it to the farmyard gas pump, this farmer filled the tank to running over.

Then he said in low German, "*Laut ons bee gohns. Dout nobat ye noch.*" (Let us go in, it is still neighboring.) He took a handful of bills out of his wallet, gave them to us, and wished us "God's blessing."

Mary and I both fought tears as we waved good-bye.

After we helped with the harvest in Oregon, there were hearty farewell scenes that we'll never forget. Some friends we'd never see again in this life.

We started making our way toward the East Coast with our faithful Dodge. Visiting churches and friends along the way, we rarely needed a motel. We stopped at one place, however, that proved to be a private retreat for Mary and me. It was a beautiful log cabin tastefully decorated with everything arranged for cooking. In those days, cookstoves had to be loaded with kindling and wood or coal. Here firewood was set in the stove with only a match needed to set it ablaze. It was a delight—and all for one dollar!

As we continued East we visited family in Herbert and Main Center, Saskatchewan, including Uncle Jake Martens and his large growing family, as well as my sister Kathryn and her husband Art. The next stop was Munich, North Dakota, visiting Mary's childhood home and some of her relatives, where Mary reminisced tearfully.

Then we went on to Hillsboro, Kansas, where we visited several churches. Wanting to see our Biola classmates Ruby and Clyde Landrum once more, we pushed our weary Dodge across the Mississippi and on to Kentucky, coasting whenever possible to conserve gas. Driving all night, we were extremely weary; but as morning dawned we noticed that there would be one more river to cross—and this river had no bridge. Heavy rains and a swollen current had carried it away. The only way to cross was on the back of a mule. When we were finally together with our friends, the discomforts of the journey and especially that last crossing were immediately replaced by the joy of reunion, jokes, laughter, and chats around the fire. We were learning that although separation, difficulty, and trials test a friendship, they also tighten bonds and deepen relationships.

We also learned much about Kentucky living in its "original flavor" with holes in the floor, windows stuffed with rags, and the jug of Kentucky butter beside the fireplace where everyone going by stops to give a few turns on the paddle.

Our last stop was in Pennsylvania where we visited my brother Jake and his wife Nada. While staying with them, we received our passports and completed last-minute packing. Then we said our last teary good-byes and set out on the last lap of our journey to New York. The Dodge was ready to give up as we limped into New York City late at night, and Mary was weepy. It no longer paid to get a hotel room, so we sat in the old Dodge on a street in Brooklyn waiting for dawn. The next day we picked up our tickets along with the visas that—to our relief—had just arrived. As soon as these errands were completed, we found an inexpensive room to stay in—our last shelter on American soil.

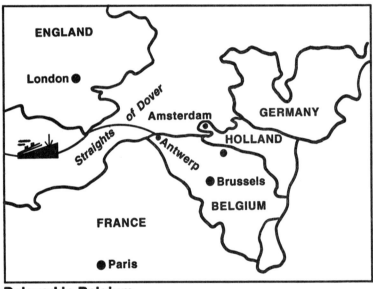

Delayed in Belgium

$\boxed{14}$

Strange Shoes in a Strange Land

Not knowing what to do, we sat on a bench.
North Atlantic Ocean
1932

At 2 p.m. February 12, 1932, the Red Star Lines finally allowed the SS *Pinnland* to pull anchor and leave the pier. It had been scheduled to sail the day before when all the passengers had boarded, but was delayed by a dense fog.

As we watched the shoreline grow smaller and smaller, we felt a few twinges of nostalgia, but also a sense of God's perfect timing in every detail. The trip across America and Canada had permitted us to see nearly all our family and friends, and make many new friends.

The old Dodge had seen us safely to New York. We even hated to let her go.

Our last two days in New York had been most beneficial. We'd been to one of New York's large churches to hear

Harry Rimmer, a Christian scientist. He spoke on the Person and work of the Holy Spirit. Encouraged by his message, we accepted it as God's "send off" to us. It dispelled the apprehension we felt as we faced our first venture.

Then, by a miracle of God's providence, we were able to get together with my old buddy Joe Brownstone from Herbert, Saskatchewan, who was living in New York. Besides spending a wonderful evening with him, we were delighted when he came to the pier to see us off.

A telegram was delivered to our cabin with a farewell message from Jake and Nada. Again our hearts were warmed by that thoughtful gesture.

After getting acquainted with our cabin and freshening up, we walked down the corridor and stepped into the ship's dining room. Bright lights lit up the linen tablecloths, napkins and elegant food. Everything seemed extravagant and luxurious. I was sure that my parents had not enjoyed such elegance on their voyage from Russia. I felt in my heart a deep sense of gratitude for them.

The next ten days we relaxed and rested while catching up on letter writing and studying. At times we wondered about the future. We were supposedly setting out for Africa, yet the money we'd carefully saved had been enough only to buy a ticket as far as Belgium. Were we acting on faith—or presumption? We decided to focus our thinking on Belgium. It was at least a step in the right direction. Besides, it was the mysterious *other* country that had strangely touched our hearts and we were anxious to make its discovery.

After the ninth day at sea we began stretching our eyes to catch our first glimpse of land. Excitement increased as the distance between us and the French shoreline decreased. Our arrival, however, was a little different from our anticipations.

The Janzens had written that, after landing in Le Havre, France, we were to take a train to Paris and then to Antwerp, Belgium, where a certain Mr. Wilson would meet us.

Passing customs was difficult and frustrating. Bumping through the crowds with baggage, standing in lines amid confused people, and trying to explain to impatient and sometimes rude customs officials was chaotic. We finally managed to board our train for Paris, though, where we had lunch before going on to Antwerp.

Our first experience of France had been rather unsettling, but as we settled back on the train winding through the towns and villages of Belgium, we were intrigued by the new sights. The first thing that caught our eyes was the workmen on the streets. They wore wooden shoes, and lunched on sandwiches nearly a foot long—or so it seemed.

After getting off the train in Antwerp at 7:30 p.m., we looked around for our Mr. Wilson, but no one seemed to meet his description or to be looking for us. We finally decided we'd better find a hotel room.

We learned the meaning of the word *strange* that first evening. The country, the language, the people—all were strange. We realized that to the people of this country, *we* were strange. Our clothes, our speaking, and even our shoes were strange. We were indeed *strangers* in a *strange* land.

The next day we were able to locate Mrs. Wilson, who told us that her husband had left her, taking with him all their savings, as well as that of many missionaries. He'd been serving as an agent booking passages and lodgings for missionaries. We then knew that we were on our own for all future arrangements. We went to a park and prayed that the Lord would lead us to a room we could rent. We couldn't afford to continue staying in a hotel.

Not knowing what to do, we sat on a bench. Eventually two ladies speaking English walked by. We stopped them and asked if they knew of a room for rent in the area. To our surprise they told us they'd seen a sign in a window saying *kamer to huur* (room to rent), just around the corner.

We went to the place they indicated and were pleased to find a tiny apartment that included a dining room, a bedroom, and cooking facilities. It even had a balcony. There was, of course, no bath. We were able to make arrangements with the landlady by speaking German, but we soon realized that in using "Platz Deutsch," similar to Flemish, we could communicate fairly well.

We settled into our little apartment on *Heteroginestraat* and soon began to feel less strange. We weren't far from the center of the city and the big market. Little did we know that this would be home for us for a year and a half.

15

Wooden Shoes on Rough Cobblestones

The clerks put newspapers in
their wooden shoes to keep warm.

Antwerp, Belgium
1932–1933

We became familiar with the quaint historic city of Antwerp, which was home for 300,000 people. It derived its name from the words *Hant werpen* or *throwing of the hand*. According to tradition, if a ship captain refused to pay toll to local pirates, the pirates would seize the ships, cut off the captain's hand, and throw it in the river.

The narrow cobblestone streets buzzed with activity. Between the rows of dark, red brick townhouses, there were few cars. Taxis honked their rubber air horns. Milk wagons drawn by teams of dogs mingled with horse-drawn bread wagons. Intricate sculptured steel lattice work on big cast-iron posts supported the huge slate roofs covering the merchandise on the docks. Big Belgian draft horses, with their thick shanks and broad muscular shoulders, pulled cargoes of beer or boxes containing minerals, diamonds, ivory tusks, and other goods that were loaded on and off the freighters at the docks. We marveled at these beautiful horses that needed to be guided only by one rein.

At nighttime, when the horses started off with their loads, the scraping of their horseshoes on the cobblestones threw streaks of sparks.

Mary especially enjoyed *Groen Plaatz,* or the marketplace. This weekly market was a living tapestry of Belgian life. The faithful dogs, which had pulled their master's wagons, waited patiently under the stands.

The clerks put newspapers in their wooden shoes to keep warm. Little pails of live coals by their feet provided meager warmth to combat the cold February winds that swept through the open area.

All kinds of merchandise were displayed, including fresh vegetables, cheese, meat, fruit, clothing, yardage, dishes, pots and pans, flowers, and various trinkets. The prices were reasonable. One of the first things we purchased was bread and butter. As Mary paid for the butter, the fat salesclerk dropped the change, which fell on her ample stomach. Speaking in Flemish she exclaimed, "If I weren't so fat I would have lost the change." To our surprise we understood everything she said.

Later, as we strolled around taking in all the interesting sights, Mary bumped into a woman who shouted, "Watch out, sleepyhead!" Again we understood exactly what was being said. Instead of being put out by the rather rude remark, we beamed with excitement. Realization had just struck us that Flemish, one of the languages spoken in Belgium, was a dialect of our *Platz Deutsch* or low German. As there are many local dialects, we'd soon be speaking the Antwerp version.

Another place we enjoyed was the pier. There we'd watch the Congo boats come in and go out. We imagined ourselves on one of those departing ships. Then we'd leave with a sigh. When would our turn come?

When snow fell the first weeks of March, we had a hard time keeping our little apartment warm. We didn't know how to operate the little coal stove. But after trying several different kinds of coal, we finally found one that produced warmth rather than smoke. In the meantime, we hugged our hot water bottle.

After visiting several churches—some English-speaking and some German—we finally discovered the *Evangelische Kerk*, a branch church of the Belgian Gospel Mission. Immediately we felt at home. The people welcomed us with enthusiasm and warmth. After the service, the pastor and his wife, Mr. and Mrs. Meyers, invited us to their house for delicious Belgian coffee.

From then on we had a standing invitation to dine in their home on Monday evenings, their only free day. We learned to enjoy *strumpf* and other Belgian dishes. What impressed us most was the prayer of thanks before—and after—meals. When everyone was through eating, Mr. Meyers would often quote a passage from Deuteronomy: "When thou hast eaten and art full, then thou shall bless the Lord thy God..." (Deut. 8:10 KJV). We found this custom quite appropriate. It's so easy to take for granted the blessings we already have. We determined to practice the same in our home after special dinners.

Little by little, friendships developed and invitations became plentiful. There were also happy times at picnics in the park and excursions up the Schelde River, to the zoo, or to the Plantin Moretus printing museum. We soon realized that the strangeness we'd felt upon arriving had vanished. Bonds of love that had no respect for difference of nationality tied us together as one family.

In due time, in spite of limited means, our little apartment on *Heteroginestraat* welcomed guests as well.

One of our guests was a sharp young woman of about 16, Elizabeth Lemière, who had a keen interest in missions. She had applied to go to Bible school but was turned down because, at that time, they didn't accept women. She listened with excitement as we told of our plans for Africa. Finally she asked, "Could I go along? I would like to see missionary activity firsthand and maybe I can help."

At first we were not a little surprised, but watching her expression we could tell that her interest was genuine. If God was leading her in this way, who were we to stop her? We agreed that if our Mission Board accepted the proposition, we would be pleased to have her accompany us. After making application with a letter of recommendation from Pastor Meyers she was immediately accepted as a full-fledged missionary. She didn't need a visa, as Congo was then a Belgian colony.

Besides doing housework, Mary was kept busy sewing clothes for Africa. We had had no opportunity to do this before leaving America, and the market in Belgium had a good selection of fabrics suitable for the tropics. Seeing how long and tedious this task was becoming, I found myself offering to help cut out and stitch. Later she helped me copy my notes from Bible school. We enjoyed working together in this way. Our sewing bee of two provided a conducive atmosphere for deep discussion and when we copied my notes, we rejoiced together in the spiritual truths and mysteries we were once more uncovering, along with many new insights. The potential such sharing can have in bonding a couple together, and the resulting sweetness, can only be known by those who are one in the flesh *and* in the Spirit.

Opportunities for service also presented themselves. Mary helped clean apartments for the older people of the church, and spent many evenings with a Madame Van Duynen who was terminally ill. We also helped, whenever there was a need, a certain couple starting a hospitality house for missionaries.

This particular house was large—as was the man's temper, while his wife was the personification of kindness. How often we heard her say, "Now Palmer, do be careful, for Satan is already loose this morning." We also witnessed memorable occasions when victories were won through confession and forgiveness. Such times were so sacred that one almost felt the need to tiptoe quietly out of the room. Another victory we were privileged to witness was a man winning over an unhealthy habit.

We were walking to church one evening when we met Mr. Lambrecht, who was employed at the large Antwerp zoo (supposedly the world's largest). He and his wife were also on their way to church. When he saw us, he jerked from his mouth the pipe he was smoking and stuffed it in his pocket. I wondered that it didn't set his pocket on fire. Prior to this we'd never discussed smoking; but no doubt, he'd observed that we didn't smoke. Strangely enough, this became the subject of our conversation and from that day on he stopped smoking. Later he confided in me that his doctor had told him that had he not stopped smoking at that time, he would have died.

16

Belgian Carpet Slippers on Hardwood Floors

It was a mingling of magical
flavorings...and cozy feet.

Antwerp, Belgium
1933

As the days stretched out our food barrel shrank lower and lower and sometimes scraped empty. Finally the day came when all that was left in the cupboard were some prunes—which we ate for breakfast. We consoled ourselves with the fact that we'd been invited to a birthday dinner that evening in the home of the Lambrechts.

Our hosts met us graciously at the door and offered carpet slippers. We later learned that this was customary in Belgian homes, for it not only provided comfort for guests, but also kept muddy shoes from tracking dirt into the living room. An extra bonus for the homemaker was that the slipping and sliding required to keep the slippers on the feet also provided the polishing that kept her floors shiny.

Our hosts then proceeded to serve a seven-course dinner that lasted for hours. It included several *hors d'oeuvres* and main dishes, then fruit, cheese, and finally cake and coffee. It was a mingling of magical flavorings, graceful serving, charming conversation, and cozy feet.

Walking home after this delicious dining experience, we felt like it had all been a fantasy dream, and as we climbed the stairs to our little apartment we were confronted with the reality of our empty cupboards. Where would our next meal come from? At the top of the stairs we spotted a white envelope on the small table where our landlady sometimes deposited our mail. In seconds I had my penknife open and the contents of the letter in my hands. In disbelief we gazed at a substantial check—enough to cover many meals.

Our greatest test came on May 21st, when a letter arrived from Africa. By then we'd already established a custom, which we maintained throughout our married life, of waiting till we were together before opening or reading personal letters. These were then read out loud, usually by Mary. On this morning we were sitting at our kitchen table where I slit the letter open with my penknife and handed the letter to Mary.

"Since it's taking you so long to come to Congo," Mary read, "maybe God hasn't sent you after all."

Mary dropped the letter on the table, laid her head on top of it, and wept. After pouring our hearts out to God, we contacted Pastor and Mrs. Meyers, who shared our anguish and perplexity. Together we decided to wait and trust, and in the meantime to occupy our minds by studying French. "You never know," he said, "God might still have His finger on the latch of that door to Congo."

At that time the study of the French language was not a requirement for service in Congo. It had not yet become the official language. However, we knew it was spoken by the Belgians governing the Congo, so it just might come in handy.

We couldn't afford to pay for language study, but a missionary serving with a Jewish mission graciously tutored us, as much as his time permitted. The process was slow because we had little opportunity to use the words we were learning.

Meanwhile, back in our hometown of Dallas, Oregon, Evangelist Peach had dropped in for another series of meetings. He asked about us and was informed that we were still in Belgium. No one seemed to know *why*. But someone suggested, "Why don't you ask Abe's parents?" This was a time in the history of missions when missionaries operated strictly on faith. Salaries and promised support were unknown, as were *prayer letters* or other *fund-raising* strategies. Needs were mentioned only in prayer or—when asked—to intimate family and friends.

Evangelist Peach went to my parents and asked, "Why are Abe and Mary still in Belgium?"

"Because they don't have enough money to pay for a ticket to Africa," my Dad replied.

"Well then, it's time to tell the church," he said emphatically. "I'll take care of that myself."

The very next meeting he challenged the congregation to send us on to Africa, and a few weeks later we received a precious envelope containing a check sufficient for a boat ticket to Africa. This time Mary and I cried and laughed with joy.

Africa at last

17

Sailing Shoes Facing New Horizons

We held in our hands the long-awaited tickets.
Atlantic Ocean—Antwerp—London—Lobito
1933

Of the 16 and a half months that we'd been in Belgium, we saw the sun only occasionally. Rain and clouds, we found, were typical of this little country on the North Sea. During those months it seemed that our path was as hazy as the weather. There were many days when we longed for a bright light to shine through, so we could clearly see the way ahead, but our finite minds were restrained. We could only wait. This is quite a test for an active, decisive person like myself. Whereas I often paced the floor or spoke impatiently to Mary, she would cringe at others' misunderstanding. "Everyone's asking us what our plans are, and I never know what to say," she'd complain.

With the passing of time one can look back at the pattern of one's footprints on the trail of life and trace a design not visible at the time those footprints were made. Later we'd marvel at God's wisdom in delaying us in Belgium long enough to learn some basic French and to establish a bond with the Belgian people. These two elements were essential in preparing us for a ministry that would surpass our wildest dreams.

Now, with the funds in hand, we booked passage for July 11, 1933. We were thrilled when we held in our hands the long-awaited tickets that would take us to Africa. Suddenly, however, it dawned on us that in leaving for Africa, we'd be saying "good-bye" to our Belgian friends, who'd become as dear as family, and to charming Belgium, which we'd unconsciously adopted.

The church gave Elizabeth Lemière and us a touching send-off after the morning service. Emotion-packed speeches were given, followed by prayers of dedication and intercession mixed with songs of praise. The church then gathered outside for a memorable picture taken by a professional photographer. Finally there was coffee with refreshments. Sorrowfully, we pulled ourselves away from tearful embraces and the triple kisses, typical of Belgian custom.

The next morning I rented a handcart. After loading all our belongings, the three of us set off across the cobblestones to the boat. A good group of friends came to the Antwerp harbor to see us off. When the boat pulled out at 2 p.m., the handkerchiefs, waving in the wind, were as the sweet breath of the Spirit filling our sails and blowing us out to sea. Our first stopping place would be London, England.

The Kingdom of Britain welcomed us in the manner that she customarily receives all her visitors—with rain and fog. The sun never came out to greet us the entire week we were there. We purchased raincoats and set out to investigate some of the interesting landmarks of London. The biggest treat was hearing G. Campbell Morgan speak at Westminster Abbey. Afterwards we ate a picnic lunch in the park and roamed the streets, stopping to watch the changing of the guard at Buckingham Palace.

Our last minute shopping was hectic. We chased all over London for helmets. In those days people going to the tropics were afraid of sunstroke. So they wore heavy, cumbersome pith helmets lined with a corklike insulation and cloth.

The last day Mary wanted to pay one more visit to Woolworth's. She felt she needed a last glimpse at civilization's comforts and soft things. That evening she struggled with homesickness and depression. Life ahead would be crude and rough for a delicate woman like my Mary, with her keen sense of beauty, creativity in dress, and skill in cooking and sewing. She knew there would be no stores where she could run in to choose a card or pick up some thread.

The only comfort I could bring was to kneel with her before our compassionate Heavenly Father, who understands the struggles we face when we seek to follow His leading. Together we renewed our commitment to God and each other. I reassured Mary that God surely had some unexpected surprises waiting for her, ones that would outweigh all she was leaving behind. When we got up, her eyes were smiling through her tears.

The next day we were most happy to get on board the Dunbar Castle, a 10,000-ton motor ship. As we left the Thames River and entered the open sea, it was without a single ripple. We were looking forward—happy to be on our way to Africa at last!

Our third class accommodations were inconvenient. The men slept on one side of the ship and the women slept on the other. The first thing we had to do was reorganize our suitcases to separate our belongings. For Mary, the lack of privacy and being apart from me was difficult. For our traveling companion, Elizabeth Lemière, however, it proved to be a little less lonely. Mary and Elizabeth shared a room with two other women and I shared a room with three men.

Another hurdle for Mary was finding her "sea legs." The combined impact of apprehension and the odor of dead fish, paint, and tobacco stole her appetite. By the time we reached the high seas, she felt desperately ill. She wanted only to retreat to the cabin. I found it necessary to drag her to the deck for a little exercise so she could fill her lungs with fresh, clean sea air. A natural sailor myself, my appetite was more ravenous than ever.

Life on the boat included parties and the type of entertainment we found disgusting. After a walk on deck, we'd often go to bed early to read or let our minds drift to friends at home, wondering when we'd hear from them.

The 24 days seemed to drag by until August 4, when at about 3 p.m. the ship docked in Lobito, Angola. We stood, almost in a daze, as we tried to take in our first sight of our promised land. Filtering through our minds was the realization that God had fulfilled His promise. The waiting and the perplexity of the 16 months in Belgium had only added to the delight of the moment—the answer to our prayers and the realization of our dreams. Our feet would soon be walking on African soil and perhaps we'd soon be telling the story of Jesus to those who had never heard. We vacillated between spurts of impatience and twinges of fear. The path before us led to the interior of the so-called *Dark Continent*, where we would not be spared encounters and conflicts with the dark forces of demonic powers and where harsh living conditions awaited us. What if we should somehow prove too small for the task? The prayer of our hearts was expressed 20 years before by Amy Carmichael:

> From prayer that asks that I may be
> Sheltered from winds that beat on Thee,
> From fearing when I should aspire,
> For faltering when I should climb higher
> From silken self, O Captain, free
> Thy soldier who would follow Thee.

From subtle love of softening things,
From easy choices, weakenings,
(Not thus are spirits fortified,
Not this way went the Crucified)
From all that dims Thy Calvary,
O Lamb of God, deliver me.
Give me the love that leads the way,
The faith that nothing can dismay,
The hope no disappointments tire,
The passion that will burn like fire,
Let me not sink to be a clod:
Make me Thy fuel, Flame of God.

Reprinted by permission of the Dohnavur Fellowship.

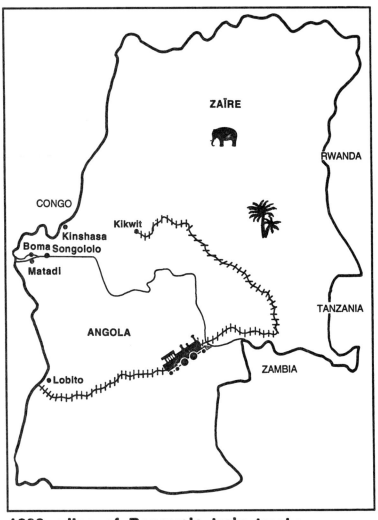

1600 miles of Benguela train tracks

18

Exploring Shoes on the Land of Dreams

The waving branches of
the palm tree beckoned us.

Lobito, Angola
1933

The humid heat was stifling as Mary and I walked down the gangplank. Sweat poured off the black, shirtless backs of the men who worked on the docks. Some were pulling on ropes or rolling big drums off the ship while others darted in and out with luggage or parcels in various sizes and shapes balanced on their heads.

The women waiting for the ship to dock stood out in their brightly colored outfits. The skirt was a large piece of fabric wrapped around the body and fastened at the waist. The top was a full, loose blouse gathered to a yoke. Short ruffled sleeves added the finishing touch to this standard style, which, with the variety of colors and designs, was as varied as the infinity of African art.

Some women wore bright bandanas tied at the backs of their heads. Several large brass anklet bands were visible on ankles and numerous strands of tiny beads in brilliant colors were worn around their necks or around the waists of their babies. Many interesting objects were used as earrings: safety pins, peanuts, shells, twigs, stones, bones, or pieces of ivory. Some had a reddish powder on their bodies, as well as on their faces and hair. Some wore well-worn tie-up shoes or sandals. Most wore none. Babies and young children bounced on hips, or in slings on the backs of mothers or older brothers and sisters who were dressed in loincloths or short wraparound skirts of fabric or woven cloth.

Unaccustomed smells filled the air. Mixed with odors of human bodies were those of fish, raffia, vegetables, fruits, and animals—particularly goats and chickens. We would later appreciate the *macayaba* (large dried fish), *luku* (a hard mush made of manioc and millet), *sukasuka* (manioc leaves), and *pilipili* (hot peppers).

We would learn to drink goat milk and to check the freshness of eggs by holding them up to the sunlight. Experience would teach us never to crack an egg directly into a bowl with other ingredients. Unpleasant surprises would quite frequently be the result if we were not careful.

In the background the palm trees stretched to the heavens, towering over the rest of the tropical foliage. The waving branches seemed to beckon us. This tree would become a symbol of all that Africa would mean to us. Now it was time to put on the proverbial pith helmet, which would mark the beginning of our missionary career in Africa.

The ship had docked in Lobito, Angola, Friday the fourth of August, 1933. Angola was a Portuguese colony quite a distance from the Belgian Congo, our designated place of service. We were disappointed, when we went to purchase a train ticket, to learn that no train was scheduled before Monday. This meant we'd have to wait a few days in Angola when we were so impatient to get to Congo. Thus we spent our first memorable weekend on the African continent in Lobito.

We soon discovered that the white people in Angola didn't speak English or French, and of course the Africans spoke other languages and dialects. Yet we will never forget our first Sunday in an African church. As we heard the congregation sing and praise the Lord, we couldn't hold back our tears. God had put a love for these people in our hearts that would remain there the rest of our lives. We longed to do our part to make the message of grace known to as many as possible on this vast continent.

We would have liked to join in the singing, but were limited both by language and by the inability to follow their rhythm. Still, we admired their enthusiasm. Ignorant as yet of the many lessons we'd have to learn, not only in language but also in codes of etiquette, ethics, and communication, we lost ourselves as we mingled our prayers of thanksgiving with theirs.

Confident that our family in America and Belgium would be thinking of us, we praised God for them as well. We were excited to see this extension of His family on another continent, proving that His love extends around the world to every tongue, tribe, and nation.

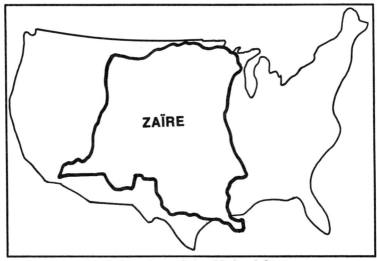

Zaire, one-third the size of the United States

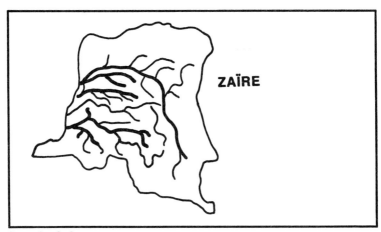

Land of rivers

19

Sooty Shoes
Initiating Service

The engine belched out smoke,
a blaze of fireworks, and soot.

From Lobito to Ilebo
August, 1933

Like many new missionaries, rather than listen to the advice of those who had gone before, we had our own ideas on how things should be done. We thought it would be more economical to enter Zaïre from the south by train, rather than through the river route suggested to us. Had we known the risks we were taking, we would have chosen the usual route that was tried and proven. The lesson we learned was invaluable, but proved costly for ourselves and others.

Zaïre,[1] a large country nearly one third the size of the continental United States, has a network of navigable rivers

---

1.   Previously the Belgian Congo

that, until the building of the railroad, provided the main source of transportation. Most missionaries, up to our time, arrived at the port of Matadi and took the train around the rapids to Kinshasa.[2] From there they would board a boat and go up river. To reach Kikwit, the town nearest our destination, they would loop around to the north, going up the Zaïre,[3] the Kasai, the Kwango, and then the Kwilu Rivers. The distance, as a crow flies, is only 250 miles, but by river spans 400 miles, taking two weeks to navigate, depending on the season.

We chose to travel on the new Benguela railway clear across Angola, entering Zaïre just north of Zambia[4] at Dilolo, and then continuing to Tenke, a distance of 900 miles. From there we took the train back northwest to the center of the country—another 700 miles. Our total trip was about 1,600 miles and we still had a distance to cover by truck at the end.

The Belgians and British had just completed the Benguela railway in 1931. It connected the rich mining area of Shaba with the coast, without having to make the long loop by riverboat. This railway carried out the copper, uranium, zinc, diamonds, and other minerals needed by the rest of the world.

The locomotive burned wood, which was plentiful along the way. It ran at an erratic pace, stopping to clear the tracks of fallen trees, make repairs, or load up wood and water. Before each grade the locomotive stopped to build up steam. When the steam pressure valve released with a big bang, the train would start chugging up the hill.

The engine belched out smoke and a blaze of fireworks, with sparks flying out the smoke stack and on all sides. Brush

---

2.   Léopoldville
3.   The largest river that is the source for the others. Previously it
       was "the mighty Congo."
4.   Previously Northern Rhodesia

along the track was ignited as the train passed by. By day the sparks were less visible, but the cinders blew back on all the passengers, covering faces with soot and burning holes in clothing. Windows, of course, stayed open for fresh air in the sweltering heat.

With their development of the area, the Belgians gave French names to the main cities such as Léopoldville—after King Leopold—Elizabethville—after Queen Elizabeth—and Charlesville—after Prince Charles. Stanleyville was named after the explorer Stanley who first set out to find David Livingstone—one of the first path-breakers into the interior of Africa. When the Africans referred to towns, they kept to the African names, while the Belgians used theirs. After their independence in 1960, the African names were used exclusively; finally, the name of the whole country was changed from Congo to Zaïre.

The Bakkongo people lived near the coast across three nations: the narrow strip of Zaïre, the Congo Republic to the north, and Angola in the south. Our trip across Angola and part of the Congo took us through some 20 of the more than 100 different tribes in this part of Africa.

Finding food along the way was a challenge. There were no dining cars on the train or restaurants at the stops. The ride, however, was interesting and acquainted us with African scenery of jungles, rivers, and plains. We were most intrigued.

Another treat was meeting some missionaries taking their children to a missionary children's school called Sakeji, in Zambia. They were jolly English people with a good sense of humor, and made our time together most enjoyable. Little did we know that we would be taking our children to the same school some 12 years later. As they stepped off the train at Kasaji we bid each other *au revoir*, the French way of saying *good-bye*. Interpreted literally, it means "Till we meet again."

At Tenke, the next stop, we had to get off the east-west train to board another train going northwest. We had a day's layover, so we stayed in a Portuguese hotel. There we were able to wash the dust and soot off our clothes, bodies, and shoes. We didn't relish the prospect of boarding another train the next day and getting all dirty with dust and heat again. Perhaps this one would be better.

Another railroad had been built running diagonally across the whole country to join the southeast mining center of Kisangani[5] with the capitol of Kinshasa. To this day, however, it hasn't been completed. Consequently, it stops in the middle of the equatorial jungle at Ilebo.[6] This 700-mile ride took us across our new country—the Belgian Congo.

As we went north toward the equator, following the flow of the rivers, we plunged deeper and deeper into the equatorial rain forests where the heat became torrid as the humidity increased. By the type of huts the people lived in, we could see that the tribes were more primitive.

This part of the train trip was even more unpleasant than the first. The excitement of the adventure began to wear down with the constant clatter of starting and stopping, along with the dust and flying cinders, not to mention the heat that drained us of energy. Each time the train stopped, the insects replaced the cinders taking over the compartment. We wondered when we'd ever reach our destination!

Eventually the train approached Port Franqui where the tracks went right down to the little river port. Here the merchandise was unloaded from the train to the Mississippi-style riverboats, to continue the trip downstream and up different rivers to other parts of the country.

We got off the train thinking we were near our destination. Less than a hundred miles by car meant only a few hours, even in our old Dodge, back in America, before the days of freeways. Now we were in another country where

---

5.   Elizabethville
6.   Port Franqui

time didn't seem to count. Schedules were just a formality. The only telephones were along the railroad and used exclusively for the trains. Mail followed the erratic train-riverboat-and-porter route. No one was in a hurry; nor could they be. The Belgian man in the little wireless office of the train station handed us a telegram. It was from Aaron and Ernestina Janzen saying that they would be coming for us in four days.

Mary and I were relieved. We had reached another milestone in our long voyage to our place of service. We had just come through the big forests by train. For some strange reason the word *jungle* was never in our vocabulary; we just spoke of the forest. Ahead of us was the huge Kasai River. A stern-wheel steamer was loading the merchandise from the train. We could see Africans paddling their canoes all around, loaded down with fish and all kinds of food.

I was delighted to get my first glimpse of an African canoe. It was skillfully carved out of a big hardwood log. In spite of its weight, it cleared the water just as well as the Indian canoes I had seen in British Columbia. Then there was a big canoe carrying about 20 people and what I estimated as over a ton of merchandise.

I kept pointing things out to Mary, who was more concerned about getting the soot washed off and finding a place to spend the night. We were so dirty, we hardly recognized each other.

We made our way up the red earth path from the primitive railroad station. Only a few people could understand our French. When we inquired about a hotel or an economical place to stay, we were told about a *sombola* that we could occupy free of charge. This name, probably of Portuguese origin, designated a guest house. The Belgians had one built in each main village to give the administrator a place to stay when he came through. Constructed from local materials, the walls were made of poles planted in the ground. Palm pole slates were tied to the poles horizontally. These were crudely plastered with red mud or clay, and whitewashed.

The roof was made of a ten to twelve-inch layer of grass known as a thatch roof. Such buildings were made without a single nail. The floors were of hardened earth. There were large doors and windows for ample ventilation. However, when the *sombola* was unoccupied—which was most of the time—the village goats and pigs made it their headquarters, with their contingent of fleas and other insects.

The Africans did not stay in the *sombola* because they preferred their cozier huts without windows and with small doors high enough off the ground so animals and chickens couldn't enter at will.

An African lad who had been watching us as we made our inquiries came and asked if he could be our "boy" for the time of our stay. His services were economical and, as we were ignorant of practical procedures in the tropics, we readily accepted. He showed his delight to our response with a smile from ear to ear, revealing two rows of pointed front teeth. He wore only a pair of what were once white shorts and no shoes. He got the wood to make our outdoor cooking fire and brought us water. However, he failed to inform us that we needed to boil the water. We would pay dearly for this carelessness. For the moment we, and Mary in particular, were grateful to be able to wash off the soot and grime.

20

Braced Shoes to Prevent Falling

The route led through villages
where tribal wars made passage difficult.
From Ilebo to Djoku Pundu

When our friends Aaron and Ernestina Janzen arrived,
we were relieved and happy. Coming to Ilebo had been a
long, uncomfortable, and dangerous trip for them in their
black Model B Ford truck. Their route had led through villages where tribal wars made passage difficult. When we realized this, we were impressed by their generous spirit in
giving of themselves to such an extent—and by the fact that
they never showed any resentment for the inconvenience
we'd caused.

After coming from Belgium with its crowded city life, we
were amazed by the vast openness of the African countryside. Deep blue and brown hills stretched out as far as we

could see. Winding in and out of the valleys was the deep green forest with tentacles reaching up into the plain as if wanting to pull the grass down to the big rivers.

Our road wound around, as much as possible, on the sides or tops of the hills away from the forests. The tall elephant grass reached up all around us, engulfing our little truck. In other places the branches of trees touched together above our narrow road. We didn't see any wildlife during the day. Everything and everyone seemed to be asleep.

We drove for hours without seeing anyone. Then we came through a dusty village. Chickens, scrawny goats, smooth-skinned sheep, and an occasional pig scurried out of our way. The driver was watching out for them while at the same time trying to keep the steering wheel from wrenching out of his hands in the sand. People and animals had cleared away all vegetation, leaving the soil a dark gray sand.

Naked children, young girls carrying babies, and some older men and boys came out from their huts or from under the shade trees to watch the passing truck. They appeared to be yelling at each other. We couldn't tell if they were hostile or friendly. "*Mundele, Mundele,*" they called.

Where were the women? we wondered.

Later we learned that the women were out in the fields turning the ground or at the river soaking their manioc, washing their babies, or getting water for the evening meal. The men were in the forest hunting or at home weaving and building. Six to 12-year-old girls carried two-year-old children on their hips. Their bodies were bent over to one side to balance the load on the other hip. Babies were carried on their mother's backs until they were weaned at about two.

The trip on the back of the truck was extremely tiring and uncomfortable. Our bedrolls, which served as our seats, provided very little padding as we bounced along the bumpy paths that could hardly be called roads. A *road* was merely a strip, a little larger than a vehicle, that had been cleared of trees and brush. The grass, which had simply been cut back by hoes, had grown back so that now it reached the hood of the car. Since a vehicle went over the road only once a week, or at best once a day, we could barely make out the tracks.

A cloud of dust followed our truck everywhere, covering our clothes and shoes, then swirling behind and filling our nostrils and parched throats. We quickly learned to take just little sips out of the water bottle. This was all there was for the entire trip. Service stations, of course, were totally absent.

The tall grass hid the many holes made by all kinds of burrowing animals and birds who were happy that someone had done a little advance work for them in clearing the sand. The flood streams, from the torrential rains of the rainy season, found no better place to flow than down the hillsides onto the freshly cleared strip called the road. So in many places the road became a ditch filled with sand and all kinds of brush.

This was before the days of four-wheel drives, wide mud tires, and big powerful engines. I had done a lot of driving, but I was amazed at the way Aaron Janzen carefully guided his little Ford pickup, with its narrow tires, around the bumps and through the gullies. We bumped our arms and shoulders on one side or the other with every twist, and every so often our heads hit the wooden roof when a bad bump escaped the careful eye of the driver.

We had to stop often to clear the grass seeds out of the radiator when the motor started heating up. When the road was dry, had been recently cleared, and conditions were good, we could get up to 30 miles per hour. That delight was short because soon we would have to jam on the brakes for a washboard section that would shake loose every bolt, a slope of the road that would put the little truck to the extreme limits of gravity, or a muddy section that we'd have to plow through, with water up to the little tin running boards.

We stopped briefly at Luebo, a Presbyterian mission station where we were graciously received. Then we continued to Djoku Pundu.[1] This mission station, where the Janzens had previously served, was operated by the Congo Inland Mission. There too we received a hearty welcome.

But by evening I began to feel desperately ill. I'd contracted tropical dysentery, probably from an amoeba in the drinking water in Ilebo. The next three days were a life and death struggle as my body rapidly became dehydrated. Although there was a doctor at this mission station, he could do little to help me. These were the days before antibiotics.

I firmly believe that, had it not been for the earnest, fervent prayers of Mrs. Janzen as she knelt by my bedside, I would not have pulled through. She was a mother who had lost a son to malaria and a daughter to the illness that was reaching out its morbid claws to me. God heard her tearful petitions on my behalf and spared me.

---

1.   Charlesville

21

River Shoes...on Uncrossable Waters

Our little vessel was thrown precariously into the rushing current.
From Djoku Pundu to Kafumba

After three days in Djoku Pundu, we decided to continue our journey, since another mission station was only a few kilometers away. The journey, which should have taken only a few hours, extended till after dark. The first day's journey had been mostly through the plains. Now we found ourselves plunging deeper into the forest.

We began to learn the procedure for crossing rivers. In this richly irrigated rain basin of Central Africa, it was impossible to go anywhere without crossing rivers. The only bridges available were made of local materials. Rickety wooden bridges were built over rivers up to about 10 meters (32 feet) wide.

I had grown up in the timberland of the Pacific Northwest where lumber was plentiful. Houses, barns, and buildings of all sizes were made of timber. In some small lumber mill towns of Oregon, even the streets were paved with lumber. Now we were in a land where you rarely saw a piece of lumber, and especially not a planed board.

We crossed bridges made of poles laid across logs that had probably been felled just at the spot of the bridge. We stopped to examine every bridge before we crossed. Everything was tied with vines. Not a nail in sight.

Sometimes the vine-wire would burst and the poles would slide apart or pile up in front of the vehicle. The truck would sit there on the big logs with all four wheels spinning freely in the air. The water kept rushing by underneath while we pushed and shoved, as if mocking our concern to make it to the next mission station before dark. It took hours of jacking and levering to get first one wheel and then the other back onto something firm.

The better bridges had some big boards tied on top of the poles. But these were limited to just one board for each tire of the truck. Here, too, driving skill was necessary to keep all wheels on the boards. Since no vehicle was present when the bridge was built, how could they know exactly how far apart to space the boards?

I was almost lifeless, my body drained and dehydrated by dysentery, and my head ached. Yet, I was challenged by the strength and skill needed to drive. Every minute new decisions would have to be made. One mistake could cause us to lose an hour of time or put our lives in danger. I longed to wrestle with the steering wheel myself and shift those gears. Would I ever be able to do this?

My delicate Mary and Elizabeth Lemière were holding on for dear life. Though brought up on a farm and accustomed to shifting hay and carrying buckets of milk, Mary had never seen anything like this. Her face was strained with tension as the vehicle swung around corners, took dips, or veered into precarious positions. She didn't try to speak, but concentrated on keeping a tight grip on the bars on the side of the truck, to keep from falling out.

From time to time she glanced my way, obviously concerned that she was unable to make me more comfortable. I could tell she was praying. As sick as I was, I was proud of my brave Mary. It wasn't till later that both of us realized that she could have been left a widow that day. How would she have managed alone in this wild country far away from friends and relatives and without means of communication? Thankfully, at the time, we were too inexperienced to realize just how perilous my condition actually was.

Our next first experience was crossing a river too wide to be spanned by a wooden bridge and too deep to be forded. We were driving along when all of a sudden the trees above our road opened up to the sky. We continued down a steep bank and locked the brakes. It was the end of the road. In front of us stretched several hundred feet of deep brown, swiftly flowing water. It appeared that our road had plunged under the water to come up on the opposite side where we could see its continuation through a clearing in the trees.

Upstream and downstream, the big trees grew right out of the water and reached up toward the sunlight. It looked as though they were trying to stop the dark, foreboding water that swirled around the trunks and branches. Further out the current was even swifter where it churned with a deep roar, unhindered by man or vegetation.

Not a soul was in sight as we stopped, but Mr. Janzen didn't seem to be worried. He just laid on his horn for about a minute. The little beep didn't seem to waken anyone other than the sand flies that jumped between our feet, or the pesty flies and other insects that buzzed around our sweaty, dirty skin. We got out and walked in different directions. Restrooms were an unknown commodity.

I looked down the river and saw the equipment for our crossing. Five big dugout canoes were spaced about three feet apart and tied together. Across the middle part were planks, placed together to form a pontoon bridge, just wide enough to drive onto with our little vehicle.

Soon men appeared out of nowhere. They were wearing dirty brown strips of raffia around their waists. Magically they produced paddles and stood facing us like soldiers. The paddles, which reached up above their heads, looked more like guns than tools. *Did they have the strength to take those boats across the rushing stream?* I wondered. I didn't relish the thought of being abandoned to the insects in this deserted place.

Then followed a period of discussion between Mr. Janzen and the paddlers. We repeatedly heard the words, "*Matabish, matabish.*" One man pointed to himself and said, "*Kapita.*" *He must be the captain of the crew,* I thought. Mr. Janzen later explained that they were bargaining on how much tip they would receive. *Palavers* was a new word in our vocabulary. Every section required hours of loud, animated discussion.

The men pulled their canoe ferry up to the landing point. Four men lifted each plank and set it between the shore and the ferry. I was intrigued by the procedure to follow, and didn't notice that Mary was walking the other way, preferring not to watch.

One African stood ceremoniously on the ferry to guide the driver. Mr. Janzen drove the little truck down the bank and onto the planks. I noticed that the first canoe took all the weight and went right down to the water level. At this point the correct procedure was to step hard on the gas so the vehicle could virtually jump up on the ferry before the first canoe started to sink.

Things didn't go well that day. The planks going between the bank and the first canoe slid apart and the front end of our truck went into the water. It sat there precariously. After more discussions and persuasion we used manpower that, in Africa, is more plentiful than horsepower. Pushing and pulling, they got the truck back on more solid ground. This time, the men held the front of the planks with their bare feet until the wheels were solidly on them. Then, while some pushed from behind, the little four-cylinder motor gave all its power. The truck jumped ahead, onto the ferry. Mr. Janzen jammed on the brakes just in time to keep from shooting right over the other side into the deep water.

There sat our little vehicle, perched on top of the canoes. Mary reluctantly got on board, and together we stood on the little available space beside the truck.

The Janzens had confidence in the strength of our paddlers. About five of them got into the canoes while others pushed with long poles or pulled on branches along the river. They pushed the ferry about 100 feet up stream along the edge. Sometimes it seemed that the branches would sweep our car off into the water.

Finally, with a yell, they pushed off from the edge. The paddles dipped straight down into the water. We could see the muscles strain as the men pulled back with all their strength. The sun glistened on their sweating backs. The *kapita* beat time with a stick on the side of a canoe. The water churned behind us as the men paddled in perfect rhythm. Our little vessel was thrown precariously out into the rushing current. It seemed like a toothpick in comparison to the power of the mighty water around us. A little change in the current could whip us around or send us endlessly downstream.

Our hearts beat harder as we continued to pray. Would the men have the strength to paddle against the current and bring us across? We heaved a sigh of relief when, at last, the ferry touched the shore just a little below our landing spot.

We now had to follow the reverse procedure over the precarious planks to get off the ferry, only this time the driver could not let go of the gas because the truck had to make it up the bank onto more level ground. The little Ford motor sputtered at first, but did its job. The ferry men lined up, and we were surprised to see their delight at receiving each a handful of rock salt from Mrs. Janzen. These corn-size grains of salt were our new currency. It was much more useful than money. The men would have to walk a day or two to reach a Portuguese or Belgian trading post where they could spend their money. The salt, however, would flavor their *sucasuca* (manioc green) or dried fish which their wives would be cooking that evening to eat with *lucu*, their mushlike bread. "*Kwenda mbote*," (literally Go Good or "Good-bye") they yelled as we jumped back onto the Ford and puttered down the endless bumpy dirt road.

How good the bed felt at Nyanga, another mission station run by the Congo Inland Mission. Once again the kind and generous hospitality was beyond the call of duty. The following day was Sunday, August 28. Although I was still extremely weak from the dysentery, the Lord gave me enough strength to give short messages in English that were translated by another missionary. It was my first opportunity to preach before an African congregation and I considered it a tremendous joy and privilege. The time of fellowship and prayer with the missionaries that followed crowned the day and thrilled our hearts.

Starting out early the next day, we reached the much dreaded Lange River. This was a difficult crossing as it required taking a ferry to the sandbank in the middle, driving across that island of sand in the middle, and then taking another ferry to the opposite bank. The dangerous part of this crossing was the chance of being stranded in the middle, a real possibility since a different tribe operated the ferries on either bank, and were at war with one another. We feared that they would take out their hostilities on us, or refuse to help us cross the river, or just give us a good scare. We were at their mercy.

As we waited for the ferry we got a nice view of the crocodiles. Some were sunning themselves on the banks of the river while others plopped back into the water and swam away. We were amazed at the little spindly-legged and long-beeked crocodile birds sitting on their backs or walking around. The crocodiles would open their mouths and the birds would pick the meat from between their teeth. It appeared to me to be a good illustration in relationships. They saw beyond each other's flaws and in spite of their diverse characters, could enjoy happy camaraderie.

It took from 8 a.m. to 4 p.m. to cross this river, but again, God sheltered us from harm and protected us from the wrath of man. With great relief we drove on.

Crossing rivers would remain, in the days to come, a major hurdle. Unlike some sports, there wasn't any sophisticated gear to guarantee protection. With time and experience we developed our river shoes, but we were never free from surprises. Like all hurdles in the life of a Christian, the armor of faith is the surest protection. Mary used to love to hum or sing:

> Got any rivers you think are uncrossable
> Got any mountains you can't tunnel through
> God specializes in things thought impossible,
> He'll do for you what no other friend can do.

We arrived at Mukedi mission station late that evening. This was another station operated by the Congo Inland Mission and most of the missionaries were Mennonite. Again our needs were met with thoughtful care.

Leaving Mukedi at 8 a.m. the next morning, we arrived early in the afternoon at Kandale mission station, which was run by a Baptist group. Here the missionaries got together and, with the help of their *boys*, served a delicious potluck dinner, but not before showing us comfortable lodging that included abundant water to refresh ourselves.

We were touched by all the hospitality shown to us along the way. In the tropics, every task is time-consuming and difficult. There are no grocery stores nearby where one can pick up whatever extra is needed to cook a company meal. Yet no mention was made of inconvenience. It appeared rather that we were doing them a favor by allowing them to entertain us. Mary and I concluded that this was what biblical hospitality was all about. We determined that, with the Lord's help, we would do the same for our guests.

After one more day on the back of the truck we finally reached Kafumba station, which was to be our base. At this station there was another couple, Mr. and Mrs. Jantz, and a Portuguese couple, Mr. and Mrs. Olivera. These three couples would become our coworkers. Mr. and Mrs. Janzen were, of course, responsible for the oversight of this station. They too were Mennonite Brethren, and unofficially linked to the Unevangelized Tribes Mission as were we.

Stiff and sore, we were thankful to have reached our destination. After a short evening meal of sweet potatoes cooked in palm oil, some wild boar meat, and some African spinach called *elephant ears*, we were more than ready to be shown our room: a storeroom for the mission supplies.

Our mattress was composed of cornhusks. As we drifted off to sleep that evening, we didn't realize that we'd be lying on those cornhusks for two weeks while our bodies fought a first bout with malaria, with our temperatures reaching 104 degrees.

22

New Shoes Breaking Into a New Life

Missionaries starting out faced the fact
that—*probably*—they'd never return.
Kafumba
1933

Though frustrated from being laid up with illness when so anxious to get started in actual service, we soon realized that, before putting on our *new work shoes*, there were some important lessons to learn. Besides dangers in river crossings, there was the susceptibility of our bodies to illness and sudden death. Malaria, amoebic dysentery, and sleeping sickness, caused by the deadly *tsetse fly*, were but a few. We were learning that certain precautions such as boiling water for 20 minutes, using permanganate to wash vegetables, and sleeping with mosquito nets, were lifesaving.

Yet, in spite of all these precautions, dangers lurked everywhere. Living in constant fear would paralyze our ministry.

There was only one cure: running to our refuge, as Psalm 91 so beautifully describes:

He who dwells in the shelter of the Most High will rest in the shadow of the Almighty. I will say of the Lord, "He is my refuge and my fortress, my God, in whom I trust." Surely He will save you from the fowler's snare and from the deadly pestilence. He will cover you with His feathers, and under His wings you will find refuge; His faithfulness will be your shield and rampart. You will not fear the terror of night, nor the arrow that flies by day, nor the pestilence that stalks in the darkness, nor the plague that destroys at midday (Psalm 91:1-6).

As strength returned, we marveled that we'd escaped the clutches of death while others tragically fell. In those early days, missions lost from 20 to 50 percent of their missionaries. Every mission station had its little garden where seeds await resurrection morning. Missionaries starting out had to face the fact that—*probably*—they'd never return to their loved ones or see their homeland again. This was vividly enacted before our eyes about a year later, as we witnessed the arrival of some new missionaries: Marcus and Marion Fritzel with daughter Ferry Anne.

After embarking from the riverboat that had arrived in Kikwit, Marcus Fritzel proceeded to carry his steamer trunk on his back, while Africans, wanting to earn a few francs, were standing by. His philosophy was, "We've come to serve them, not make them wait on us." When he arrived at the missionary guest house, bone weary and exhausted, Mary, who was watching him with concern, remarked, "Mr. Fritzel, if you carry on like this, you're going to die."

To this he replied, "That's what I came for!"

A few months later news reached us from the Shambungu station that Marcus Fritzel had died of malaria. Some might call him careless and irresponsible. Others can affirm that he fulfilled his life's ambition and left a stronger impact on Africa than some of the rest of us. "Victories of the church lead over the graves of many of her members," wrote John Ludwig Krapft, two months after his arrival in Africa in 1844, and following the death of his wife and baby. The African Church has been rich in such victories, and many valiant warriors have not even had the dignity of burial and a gravesite.

Once strength returned, Mary and I explored beautiful Kafumba station, which abounded with shade from the numerous palm trees. A grove of lemon, orange, and tangerine trees filled the air with pungent fragrance. Farther down the hill was a banana grove where enormous clusters hung amid massive leaves of rich green. Shrubs and bushes thrived beside the walks and around the houses.

We were also impressed with all the activities being carried on, and by their scope. Besides the church services, there were daily Bible studies, some of which were led by the Africans. A compound provided lodging for the students, many of whom were married.

Obviously Mr. Janzen, besides being a first-class safari chauffeur, had the gift of administration. His program included evangelism, discipling, and training teacher-evangelists, whom he also supported through a palm oil industry. Because of the Depression, funds from America were hardly adequate for their own needs, much less those of African evangelists. Besides a strong faith, Mr. Janzen's ingenuity, perseverance, and hard work had led to the opening of Kafumba and were now evident in the growth of this strategic station.

In charge of this "tent-making" aspect of the station was a Portuguese couple, Mr. and Mrs. Olivera, who had originally come to work with a Portuguese trader in Kikwit. Through their friendship with the Janzens, they'd come to a personal relationship with Christ, then offered to be of service.

The whole valley where the Mission was located was full of tall, oil-producing palm trees. The trunks of these trees had jagged edges from branches that were cut off as the trees grew up. The Africans were very agile in climbing these trees, then, while leaning against a belt, they would swing their machetes, cutting down palm fruit under the top branches. This was extremely dangerous as a wrong move with the machete could cut off the narrow fiber belt holding them. Such accidents did occur, but thankfully not at Kafumba. Once the palm fruit was cut down, it took only a simple procedure of heating the palm kernels, putting them through hand-turned presses while collecting the oil, and finally selling the oil.

Being young in the faith, the Oliveras lacked some of the disciplines that come with maturity, but we enjoyed good times of fellowship with them. At one time, we were together for dinner after which we had devotions and a time of sharing. In frank honesty Mr. Olivera exclaimed, in his Portuguese French, "*Moi, je manque la patiencé, mais ma femme manque l'intelligencé*" (Me, I lack patience, but my wife lacks intelligence).

Since Mary and I didn't know the language and lacked experience, we determined to help the Janzens in whatever way we could. Thus Mary cooked and cleaned so Mrs. Janzen could be free to do other things.

It also became Mary's responsibility to oversee breakfast preparations. This included opening the doors of the house so the Africans could come in and start working.

The first morning, as she walked through the door, she heard someone say "*Bonjour.*" Jerking herself around, she found herself face to face with a big colorful parrot, who then proceeded to sing, "Don't stop praying!" then stopped abruptly.

She was told later that this was a daily performance of this parrot. The Janzens had attempted to teach the bird the song that included the phrase, "Don't stop praying, the Lord is nigh," but Mr. Parrot chose his own stopping place. He also learned everyone's name, except Ernestina Janzen's.

Stubborn as he was, he refused to give her the satisfaction. Sometimes he would repeat things we'd say, in whatever tone we'd used: scolding, loving, or humorous. The day Aaron Janzen butchered a pig, the parrot mimicked—loudly—the squealing of the pig all day long!

Mrs. Janzen was extremely busy in the care of some mulatto children, the abandoned offspring of Portuguese fathers and African mothers. She also carried on medical work, assisted by Eva Jantz. These women were not registered nurses; their services developed from emergencies. Mary accompanied Mrs. Janzen to assist her with her village medical cases, getting her own medical training from firsthand experience. In many cases where knowledge was lacking, wisdom was given following urgent prayer. For many cases, prayer was the only recourse. No amount of training, medicines, or equipment could have helped.

With insufficient medicines, Mrs. Janzen used the most common remedies, including large doses of quinine for malaria. For coughs and bronchial problems, surprisingly common in the tropics, she made her own excellent syrup by mixing castor oil, lemon juice, palm oil, and hot peppers. Castor oil was one product she kept in large supply.

One day when Mr. Janzen and I were leaving for the trading post at Kikwit, Mrs. Janzen handed us a bottle she thought was of palm oil. This was used in the place of oil or margarine. As I was the chief cook and bottle washer whenever we made a trip together, I fried some eggs in a generous amount of this oil. I didn't realize—until returning home—that there is a vast difference between castor oil and palm oil!

As the nearest dentist was two to three days away by car, it was fortunate that there was a forceps on our station for pulling teeth. This responsibility fell on me. I proceeded only after much prayer and my method, I'm afraid, was far from the *painless Parker* method.

I accepted more readily repair jobs of various kinds. Some were quite challenging. One of these was putting in new bearings and installing a new crankshaft in the old four-cylinder Chevy truck. I was fortunate to have brought out a Dyks Auto Repair manual.

This truck had seen many miles on African roads. One of the safaris in which it had served was to take two ladies from the Unevangelized Tribes Mission home office on a tour of the mission stations under their direction. This included Miss Alma Doering, the founder and secretary, and Miss Dunkelberger, the treasurer.

Both these ladies, we might say, were pleasingly plump. Thus the two of them, along with their chauffeur, Mr. Janzen, barely squeezed into the cab, which had no doors. Doors were not considered a necessity in the tropics. At one point, the truck had been without service long enough to allow some lizards to establish their homes in the cab. When frightened, lizards have a habit of dropping their tail, which then continues to wiggle. When a lizard dropped his tail into Miss Doering's neck, she went through an aerobic exercise that almost shoved Mr. Janzen out the other side. Since he was in an area where he could not stop without getting stuck in the sand, he drove on. I wish that truck could talk. It would have many a tale to tell.

As soon as the natives found out that I could repair their muzzle loader guns, the only kind the government permitted people other than soldiers to have, I had no end of clientele. The flintlocks usually needed some filing, adjustment, and oiling, which was quickly done. These guns were often used for deer or elephant hunting. To kill an elephant, the hunters would shove a sharp spears into the muzzles of their guns, run up to the side of an elephant, give a loud shout, and as soon as the elephant turned his head—aim for the heart. Then they'd run and climb a tree. I admired their graceful dexterity and can affirm that the elephants were not wasted. One elephant would provide food for a village for months.

It even appeared from time to time on our table, though I never hunted for them—or found them tasty.

Mary soon inherited the task of teaching reading skills to the adult women who'd come to the station. These same women would then stay for the afternoon doing odd jobs for which they were paid in measures of salt or dried fish and sometimes pieces of cloth, which helped their living conditions. The first time Mary assumed her responsibilities, she asked one of the women, "*Nki Nkombo na nge,*" to which she got a response of loud laughter from the entire group. Instead of saying, "*Nki Nkumbo na nge*" (What is your name?), she'd said, "What is your goat?" Her new shoes needed some breaking-in humor.

She enjoyed teaching these women to read and telling them Bible stories—at first through translation, and then in Kituba, the trade language. As she became better acquainted she could appreciate each woman. This gave birth to mutual respect and grew into trust.

How much these women did for beauty—and at what price! They tattooed their bodies, sharpened their teeth, braided their hair in tiny braids—which was an all-day job. How they could sleep with some of the live elements lodged in their hair was always a mystery to me.

Of course, the men prided themselves in their own style as well. Their hair was dressed with a special mud, and then attached to a large frame with metal tacks. They also tattooed their bodies and sharpened their teeth. But it was the women who bore the heavy loads, literally and figuratively. They would sometimes carry up to 20 pounds on their heads, including large gourds of water, wood for their cooking fire, produce from their fields, and so forth. This of course, required perfect posture and graceful walk.

We sympathized with them in their hard labor. Many would work long hours in the fields while babies bounced on their backs. They would cultivate manioc, corn, millet, and peanuts, using their sole agricultural machinery: a short-handled hoe with a long blade, crudely made by the village blacksmith. With their backs bent over, they'd swing their hoes in a crisscross fashion, often in rhythm with an African tune. Beating their manioc and millet and cooking on an open fire were more back-breaking and exhausting tasks. Here again we marveled at their rhythm and gracefulness. In one tribe, all the women used elephant tusks for mortar sticks, but in this tribe they used large, heavy poles.

Custom didn't permit wife or children to eat with husband, but woe to the husband who drank too much water that his wife had carried a long distance from the river. A man once came to us for treatment on his finger, which had almost been bitten off by his wife. Though women usually had the rough end of the bargain, their sharp, pointed teeth gave them a little leverage at desperate moments.

The men spent most of their days sitting in the shade discussing dowries and exchanging village gossip, while smoking their gourd pipes. The payment of a dowry for a wife was estimated by a woman's ability to work. Polygamy, of course, was prevalent. Sometimes a woman would prefer this, as it reduced her cultivation chore to a much smaller field.

Neither of us took formal language study. The Kituba language was relatively simple to learn, since the vocabulary was limited to about 400 words. This we assimilated with little effort. In a short time I was able to accompany Mr. Janzen on evangelistic tours in the villages and permitted to speak from time to time.

When Eva Jantz was called to another mission station, Mary took on the dispensary work, helping to care for the sick on the mission station, especially maternity cases. This increased her workload considerably.

One weekend, when all the other staff was gone, a woman was carried in by her relatives. They never came back again to see her. We surmised that she'd been cursed by the witch doctor—a cause for fear among relatives. In spite of our efforts, she died quite suddenly. As bodies must be buried the day of death in the tropics, our young cook and I made a grave, wrapped her in bamboo mats, according to custom, and lowered her to her final resting place.

We realized anew what power God's archenemy has in that land where animism, fetishism, sorcery, witchcraft, and superstition are prevalent. People live in constant fear of grieving the spirits. In order to appease those spirits, baskets with food are set out, especially by mothers when making their gardens.

The *tsetse fly* was a fearful enemy for them as well. Though easily recognized by their crossed wings and ziz-zag flying, they are skilled attackers. One can well understand why the Africans would curse when bitten by one. So many have seen their relatives taken in death as a result of their sting. For this reason, the Belgian government insisted that villages be moved from the riversides to the forest or, if possible to plateaus. The tropics have their attractions, but also their tragedies.

Our hearts went out particularly to the old who, for fear of grieving the evil spirits, were abandoned, deprived of necessities, and left to die by themselves.

Going to the village one Sunday morning to visit some of these people, we found an old mother covered with ashes and wailing. She stood beside the remains of her house that had just burned down, saying, "*Mpi a mes, mpis a mes*" (My cloth, my cloth), meaning her burial cloth. This is a woven cloth of the finest weave that one presents to the spirits at death.

Had she only known the truth of the hymn *Rock of Ages*: "Nothing in my hands I bring, simply to thy cross I cling." One hardly knows how to break through that barrier of superstition.

If we would try to bring comfort to old people by giving them a blanket to keep them warm in the chilly nights, it would be taken away by their relatives. As a result, the older folk would build fires under their beds in their tiny crude huts. Their beds were made of poles covered with a bamboo mat, and a short wooden log was used for a pillow.

Later we were saddened by reports of Timothy, the dedicated pastor of the Kafumba church, who had served so loyally and faithfully for many years. In his sunset time his family had taken nearly everything out of his house. Heathen customs can be extremely cruel.

We hadn't been on the station very long when the natives began sizing us up to see what they would call us. Sometimes these names bore history, as in the case of state officials. They were called *Bula Matadi* (Rock Breakers) after Stanley, who broke rocks on the rapids of the Congo River, south of the capital Kinshasa (Léopoldville). One of our state officials was called *Ngulu Mingi* (Many Pigs) because he tried to encourage the Africans to raise many pigs to compensate the scarcity of meat.

The Africans would eat any kind of meat, including rats or snakes, but never frogs. "The frogs are to the Egyptians—and the Africans—an abomination until this day." However, meat became more plentiful in the dry season, which was also hunting season. They hunted by building circles of fire, then digging deep trenches around them.

They called Mr. Janzen *Amerikani*, the name for the strongest and most essential cloth, as he frequently purchased this fabric at the trading center. Mrs. Ernestina Janzen was *Mama Nkende* (Mother Love); Mr. William Jantz was *Ndeke Fioti* (Little Bird), as he had been interested in the bird life in Africa and frequently asked about some bird he'd noticed; Mrs. Fannie Jantz was *Mama Nkese* (Mother Happiness); Eva Jantz was given the name *Mama Munganga* (Mother Doctor); Martha Hiebert was *Mama Lemvu* (Mother Grace); and Elisabeth Lemière they called *Mama Sodise* (Mother Helper), as she was a helper to all.

They named me *Mayele* (Wisdom), which I found embarrassing. I can only surmise that they chose such a name because I could repair and build things or because I took time to listen to their heartaches or talk about the mysteries of the "Great God." Mary's name was *Mama Mbote* (Mother Star); they had soon noticed that she had an optimistic nature, winning the hearts of many. She still is—always looking for spring in the dead of winter; seeing the silver lining on clouds and rainbows in the rain. Often, when facing a weary heart, there's a word of encouragement on her lips.

Although happy to be fully occupied with the task God had given us, we were repeatedly tried with illness, particularly Mary. Besides bouts with malaria, she developed large, painful boils, sometimes as many as nine on one arm. There were days when I feared for my *Mama Mbote* and that our term of service would be cut short. How often we sought refuge under the shelter of the Almighty wings and implored protection from the "deadly pestilence." But we had yet to experience other dimensions of that Psalm and of God's immeasurable power in our weakness.

23

Reckless Shoes Plunging Ahead

We'd barely started rolling
when a lion darted across the path.
Kamayala
December, 1933

Mary and I were overjoyed when we discovered that we were to become parents. We anticipated the event with optimism and faith, in spite of the fact that the nearest doctor was several hundred kilometers away. We reasoned that if a black child could be safely born in Africa, so could a white child. By now Mary had delivered a considerable number of babies. Confident that we knew the necessary procedures, we refused to dwell on potential problems. However, adjusting to the tropics and fighting malaria and allergies had taken a toll on Mary's health. Had Mary benefited from professional prenatal care, this probably would have been pointed out to us. I would learn that there is a fine line between faith and reckless presumption. Sometimes faith rushes in where angels hesitate. The experience we were about to go through would cause me, as the leader of my household, to consider and plan more carefully, especially where the well-being of my family was concerned. It would also inspire in me an awesome recognition of a Heavenly Father whose wisdom and power to protect and deliver surpasses that of any earthly father.

While Mary's waistline was widening, we had a visit from Bertha and Mary Miller, two missionaries who were also sisters. They were just returning from furlough. Along with them came a registered nurse, Miss Vera Rumberger, who was arriving for her first term of service. They were appointed to the Kamayala mission station. In the course of our conversation they mentioned the need for a chapel on the Kamayala station, and asked if I could come and build it. As an added incentive, they reminded us that Vera was a capable nurse and that she could tend to Mary and our soon-to-arrive baby.

I accepted reluctantly since I had never built anything, least of all with local materials.

Because riding in a truck on African roads is not the most comfortable means of transportation for a mother-to-be, I was grateful when a missionary, Mr. Bort from the Chambungu station, offered to take Mary, along with Elizabeth Lemière, in his car. I arranged to follow in the Chevy truck with Charles Whittaker, a missionary with the Unevangelized Tribes Mission who was preparing to leave for furlough. He was to be replaced by these two sisters, Mary and Bertha Miller, whose outfit had just arrived and needed to be transported to Kamayala.

Sometimes the "outfits" that missionaries brought contained almost everything except what was necessary. Problems evolved when these outfits included luxuries that made the differences between African-European cultures more evident. In those years, the information communicated to new missionaries was minimal.

However, this particular outfit contained a large amount of medical supplies that were urgently needed.

We traveled at night because our road led across long hot plains. My partner was able to doze off with his pith helmet beside him. These helmets we later named the "Congo Fetish."

We had stopped to check the oil when Charles noticed that his helmet had rolled out. He was much concerned and decided to go back and find it. I didn't want him to go on foot alone, so I decided to accompany him. About a kilometer down the road we finally retrieved the helmet.

After getting back into the truck, we had barely started rolling when an adult lion darted across our path. Both of us froze, but to our relief, the lion disappeared in the tall grass. We proceeded cautiously in our doorless truck with hearts thumping loudly and eyes straining the darkness. No lion came in view. If God can shut the mouths of lions, He can also detour them from the path of His children.

When it came to wildlife, we had determined to live together as peacefully as possible. From time to time a deer would provide some meat, so scarce on our table, but we avoided hunting expeditions. Some missionaries, however, needed this type of diversion.

Sometimes missionaries chose to go buffalo hunting. This was a particularly dangerous recreation because hunters who think they're chasing a buffalo often forget that buffaloes charge by running in circles. Thus when the hunters think they're chasing a buffalo, the buffalo is actually chasing them.

One time two missionaries from the Kamayala station were hunting buffaloes. One of them shot and wounded a buffalo which came charging down the hill. Fortunately, a small tree stood in the buffalo's path and broke the impact. The buffalo fell on one of the missionaries, knocking him over and landing sideways on his chest. The other missionary somehow lost his shoes, but managed to clear his rifle from the brush and gave the buffalo a fatal shot. Had it not been for the little tree—and those guardian angels—there would have been two widows at Kamayala that day.

While waiting for our big event at Kamayala, I set about building the chapel with limited tools and technique. We sent Africans to the river to cut down tall, straight trees that, once they were peeled, could serve as poles. This process gave us many opportunities to interact with this primitive *Chokwe* tribe.

One young lad showed me his skill in carving a fetish, or idol, with his pocketknife, the tool that every lad held hidden in his loincloth. This led to a long talk about the *one true God*. It became my prayer that the lad would never need to make another idol.

That particular day was marked in my memory since it was the day for the final stage of our building program: putting on the grass roof. This was an art I had not yet mastered. It involved cutting down the tall grass and weaving or *sewing* it onto the rafters. Not one nail was used. Later I would put up many such roofs with more expertise and skill.

The Miller sisters seemed quite satisfied with their chapel, which relieved me much. Meanwhile the arrival of our baby was coming due. Mary was getting a little concerned about some of the practical aspects, and particularly by the fact that there were no clothes for the baby.

We were sure that the mail could bring no solution to our problem. It took two months for mail to reach us, and delivery was only once a month. So we were surprised to hear from the Belgian state post at Kahembe that a package had arrived for us from America.

We were thrilled when we noticed that the customs declaration indicated a *layette*. But how could we come up with the 800 francs, then about $21, required by customs? Mary and I had strong principles about borrowing money. We had previously decided that our policy would be "owe no man any thing" (Rom. 13:8 KJV). So we prayed.

God gave Mary some inventive ideas. She decided she could market some of our possessions. So she gathered together some of the clothing we could do without. This included a few of her dresses and a pair of my pajamas. She even included some small remnants her mother had thoughtfully sent along. We then invited the Africans to take a look at our special bargains, which were quickly scooped up.

The following Sunday morning at church we recognized a number of Mary's dresses, my old pajamas, and the remnants that one had made into a Joseph's coat of many colors. What we collected from those unique sales gave us just enough money to pay the duty for our layette.

The big day finally arrived on December 18. When complications developed, I went into another room to pray. That hour, as I agonized for Mary and my child, I sensed God's nearness and restored peace. Suddenly, above the sound of the roaring lions in the nearby hills, the cry of an infant announced that our son had arrived.

I rushed into the "delivery room" and found that our baby was strong and healthy, but that Mary was hemorrhaging profusely. Vera was doing her best, but felt that a doctor was needed. I immediately set out for Kikwit, a day's journey away, to fetch a doctor. Driving all night by myself, I wished I could have smoothed and straightened the road so that the old truck could pick up racing speed.

Returning two days later with an Italian doctor, I was bracing myself for the worst when the ladies came running to meet me saying all was well and that the doctor was no longer needed. It would mean another two days journey to take the doctor back to Kikwit, but all that mattered right then was that God had spared Mary and given us the gift of a healthy son. As Mary and our baby slept side by side, I thanked God for His undeserved grace in the safe arrival of my little son. Those tiny feet would soon be wearing tiny shoes, and eventually would grow to walk in my shoes.

One of our first visitors, after Clement's arrival, was Miss Esther Bodine. Soon after coming in she heard a noise. Going to the screened window she felt a warm breath on her face. Turning around, she glanced out the window and found herself looking into the eyes of a leopard whose paw was on the screened window. With a startled jump she pulled away from the window. The leopard must have decided—or an angel told him—that he wasn't welcome because he slowly backed off without even leaving a card.

The next morning the chief of the tribe, with a leopard skin around his neck—the typical symbol of authority—came to the door with a basket of eggs. After our rather lengthy exchange of greetings, our notable guest told me, "I have come to name your child. He must have my name, as he is born on my territory. I am *'Kamakashishi.'*" We thanked him politely.

Although this name was not registered on our son's official birth certificate, it was registered in our minds. In the days to come we would use it for emphasis and for fun.

The name Clement had been my choice. Reading Philippians 4 one day, I noticed that Clement was mentioned, along with others, as *coworkers* of the apostle Paul, "whose names are written in the book of life" (verse 3). It was what we desired most for our son.

We didn't choose a second name. To me *Clement* seemed sufficient in itself. However, as I held my son in my arms, played with him, and took him for walks, I couldn't keep from calling him my *Buddy*. This name stuck and, of course, was shortened to *Bud* as he grew older. It would become his official name when addressed by English-speaking people, while the French would hold to *Clément*.

It was a grand day when the Africans heard a truck and shouted "*camion*" (truck). It was Mr. Janzen; he had come to take us back to Kafumba. It was good to see the old house again and to settle down to a number of chores and repairs while showing off our son to the missionaries and Africans.

We were glad to see that the driver ants had not called and that the mud floors had been kept hard with water. However, we noticed that the elephants had been over to relish our sweet potatoes near the house. They had literally taken out the whole field and left nothing behind but deep holes.

The following night Mary awoke to tend Buddy. She thought it strange that a verse of Scripture should suddenly come to mind. It was Luke 10:19: "Behold, I give unto you power to tread on serpents and scorpions, and over all the power of the enemy: and nothing shall by any means hurt you" (KJV). That Saturday morning as our boy Setefan swept the dirt floor, he removed the mat beside Mary's side of the bed and found a poisonous snake Mary had unknowingly stepped on in the night. Again we thanked God for His protection and for His angels.

24

Floppy Shoes With Startling Strength

In spite of treatments at Kikwit,
Mary's health continued to deteriorate.

Kafumba
1935

Mary's health was becoming cause for increasing concern. Boils on her arms and legs were making it difficult for her to get around. "Now I understand how Job felt," she'd exclaim as she attempted to accomplish her duties. I found it necessary to take her to Kikwit for treatment.

Thankfully Setefan, our house boy, was a big help and encouragement to her at this time. One of the first things Mary had taught him was to boil water a full 20 minutes so it would be safe for drinking. Another lesson she'd taught him was a thorough washing of the rice, one of the main staples of our diet. In our area ordinary potatoes were rare and too expensive for our budget. The rice, she explained, had to go through several washes before it could be cooked because it had been pounded by mortars that were not always clean. These mortars were sometimes overturned by the goats or pigs or had been walked over by the chickens.

One day the manager of the oil company store at Kikwit, where Mr. Janzen usually made his purchases, by some clerical error received a large shipment of puffed rice. None of the British or Belgian staff knew the food value of this strange cereal. The manager said to Mr. Janzen, "What am I going to do with this stuff? Can you use it?" Thus Mr. Janzen received the whole shipment. This puffed rice was in large sealed tins; so to our relief it was protected from the vermin that abounded around us. What a treat it was.

The first time Setefan brought it to the table, though, Mary was away for treatment, we wondered what in the world he was serving us. He explained that he had carefully followed Mary's instructions to "wash the rice."

In spite of repeated treatments at Kikwit, Mary's health still continued to deteriorate. It was aggravated by oozing eczema on her feet and hands and, worst of all, on her head. The doctor suggested shaving her hair. So it was with a sorrowful spirit that I performed the operation of removing her beautiful amber hair.

Frustration increased for Mary as she was unable to perform tasks expected of her; she feared she was disappointing those who had counted on her to relieve their heavy workload. Caring for my ailing wife was stressful, not only because of the time it required, but also from a sense of inadequacy in doing what was right for her, and the very real possibility that I might lose her.

When the family back home realized that Mary was in no way improving, they suggested we return to America to recuperate. This was a severe blow. We wanted so much to give ourselves for Africa. Yet we had to admit that Mary was now unable to help with the medical work and with the women who came to the station, while frequent trips to Kikwit took us away from the work. We were becoming more of a burden than a help.

We continued to wait on the Lord for guidance and finally made the wrenching decision to take a leave of absence. With sadness we faced the task of packing while questions poured into our minds. Why, after waiting so long to reach Africa, were we so soon being torn away? Eventually our hearts filled with confidence that God, who had brought us this first time, could bring us back.

After difficult farewells, Mr. Janzen took us to the Kikwit trading post. There we boarded a palm fruit boat to Leverville. The Lever Brothers operated a mill for palm oil in this place, known there as H.C.B. (*Huileries du Congo Belge*). We waited in Leverville for a stern-wheeler oil carrier to take us to the capital of Léopoldville. The time there stretched out to several weeks, but proved beneficial.

Most of the employees of H.C.B. were educated, English-speaking people from either Britain or the Gold Coast, now known as Ghana. We stayed in one of the quite comfortable furnished houses that H.C.B. maintained for their personnel. Leverville was an interesting little town with stores where one could purchase most British products not available in Kikwit—but it had no church. When it became known that missionaries were staying there, we received many visitors. Ladies brought us tea trays with assorted cakes and cookies. Others came just to be friendly. We went for walks and enjoyed each other's company.

Some of our callers from the Gold Coast were Christians, and they asked if I would conduct services. They constructed a makeshift church that looked like a large booth with bamboo poles and palm branches on the top. In that simple construction God made His presence sweet through the joy of worship, fellowship, and openness to the truth of His Word. After the service, several people made requests for baptism. So with joy, I conducted a special service by the river's edge.

Mary and I were overjoyed at the response of these enthusiastic people, so hungry for knowledge of God. We were amazed that God would use such weak vessels as us.

One day a lad, who came to visit, showed us a Kituba Bible that he carefully carried in a bag. He had been introduced to the gospel at a Baptist mission station further down the river. I asked him if he were God's son, to which he enthusiastically replied, "Yes."

Testing him further I asked, "How is it that you are God's son? I understand that God has only one Son."

"That is true," replied the lad with a smile, "but I'm His little brother!"

Spontaneously I reached out both hands. Both of us understood the sign of wholehearted greeting that also confirmed our brotherhood.

Another lad came by one day with vegetables to sell. Immediately we began talking about eternal things, which he seemed quite open to hear. He listened carefully as we explained God's great grace in offering pardon for all our sins. When he understood that this free gift was being offered to him, he wanted to accept the offer on the spot.

Later the missionaries at Kafumba wrote that he'd come to the mission station with a clear testimony and asked to be baptized. A month later, after becoming critically ill, he left this life to enter the presence of the God of all grace. I realized anew that there is no off season for discussing matters of the soul. God, in His love and grace, causes paths to cross where He can use His children to point the way to the heavenly city. Like Philip, who joined the path of the Ethiopian, we always need to be in God's appointed place and to be bold to speak the words the indwelling Spirit of God leads us to say.

The delay in Leverville came to an end with the arrival of the stern-wheeler. So much had happened in those weeks that had drawn us close to the people. Although we'd looked forward to moving, we now felt twinges of heaviness. Saying "good-bye" in any language is one of the hardest phrases to express. The closeness of God's family makes pulling apart even more wrenching, but "good-bye" is never final. Someday joy will triumph in a happy reunion that will last forever.

The down-river boat trip was not the most comfortable. Our cabin, just above the boiler, steamed with relentless heat as frequent stops were made to pick up the firewood that kept the old boilers boiling. These ancient stern-wheelers, which in the good old days had once served on the Mississippi River, were now fulfilling their second career on the Congo rivers. We wondered that they had once set the scene for romantic novels and sophisticated living. Now, with the heat and swarming mosquitoes, the charm had long since worn off. Mosquito nets were provided, but were of little benefit because they too had seen better days.

Since sleep was almost impossible, I would go out on the deck for my first spiritual meal of the day. During those times I would wonder just what the Lord was preparing for us.

One early morning I stood on deck communing with God while the first rays pierced the sky. A clear vision seemed to emerge, although I hesitate to mention it as such outside of Africa. Africans have no problem with this terminology. Those who later volunteered to keep watch over my family during my absences when I had been on prolonged evangelistic trips in the villages were able to tell the night before—by vision or dream—the day I was returning home. There were, of course, no telephones or other means of communication.

The vision was of literature: Literature that would be put into the hands of all the people in all the villages that floated across the horizon of our landscape. Literature that would speak their language clearly and point to the Savior, who loved them and desired a relationship with them. Literature that would continue to teach after the departure of the missionary. Literature that would help them to distinguish truth from error and inspire them to follow in the footsteps of Christ.

We had noticed that, due largely to the literacy efforts of missionaries, Africans were becoming literate. If only good literature could come before the harmful kinds. What an impossible dream.

Later the Lord confirmed this vision as I read from the book written by the prophet Habakkuk. Paraphrasing it from a French version, it read, "Write the vision and make it plain so that the one who reads it will understand...If it's realization is delayed, wait for it. It will surely come" (See Habakkuk 2:2-3).

We would wait for 25 years for the fulfillment of that vision. Our little son Kamakashishi, who was taking his first steps on the stern-wheeler on this Kwilu river, would take a leading role in this literature venture on a scale even wider than to African villages. Mary's floppy shoes, touched by a compassionate Hand, would also hold up for countless more miles.

25

Elastic Shoes...
Expanding With Trust

"I should have asked for $100,000;
don't limit God as I did."

American Continent
1936

In Léopoldville we stayed in the spacious Union Mission House and enjoyed rich fellowship with the missionaries coming in and going out. We then continued by train to Matadi where we boarded the Belgian steamer, the *Elizabethville*, and sailed for Antwerp, Belgium.

It was like coming home to be once again with our Antwerp friends. They were anxious to hear about the work in Africa and news about Elizabeth Lemière. We visited in many homes where the bonds between us tightened several notches.

We went to the Belgian tropical medical school in Antwerp for a thorough checkup. They seemed pleased to get a few new specimens to study. With their microscopes they found that Mary had several kinds of tropical skin diseases, but assured us that a change of climate, rest, and a good diet would have a good effect upon her.

We purchased warmer and more suitable clothing since it was now December, which, in Africa, is the hottest time of the year. Mrs. Lemière and her daughter-in-law got out their knitting needles and furiously knitted some warm outfits for Buddy, which they completed in one weekend.

We were now ready to board the *Alex van Opstal*, a Belgian freighter that was making its maiden voyage. This freighter allowed a maximum of 12 passengers, for whom they offered excellent service. It proved to be a fine and refreshing voyage in spite of the seasickness that could be expected when one crosses the Atlantic in midwinter.

Our arrival in New York was uneventful. There was no one to meet us. We collected our meager baggage and walked across the gangplank to set foot once again on American soil. About an hour later we found ourselves on a train speeding toward Philadelphia.

As the train pulled into the station, we saw Miss Doering waving to us from the other side of the tracks. Not aware of the exact time of our arrival, she was on her way to another engagement. Telephones and telegrams were not used to the extent that they are today. She shouted across the tracks, telling us to cross the street to the Mission house where she would join us for supper.

At the house Miss Dunkelberger greeted us in a matter-of-fact way. We feared that we were intruding on her busy schedule. She simply took us to a sitting room and told us to wait for Miss Doering. However, when the housekeeper, Mrs. Schlansky, found out that we were there, she came to greet us with the warmth of a sister. Verses of Scripture poured from her mouth as she reassured us of the Lord's leading and blessing on our lives.

That evening during dinner Miss Doering suggested that we buy a car, and gave us some addresses of homes where we could stay on our journey cross-country. The next day we purchased a used Chevy, and a few days later we began our journey to the West Coast. We felt the cold intensely in that car. How thankful we were for the knitted garments our friends in Belgium had so lovingly made for our Buddy.

We made as few stops as possible, but the homes we did visit were choice. One was in Pennsylvania with the parents of the Miller sisters from the Kamayala mission station. Another in Ohio, was that of the Hages. Here their daughter Ruth, who was preparing to go to Africa as a missionary, eagerly soaked up everything we had to say. We had no way of knowing that her life would result in many years of dedicated service and that her coworker, Irene Farrell, would become one of Congo's martyrs. The Millers and the Hages both showed us the most generous and kind hospitality, and we were grateful to be able to catch up on diaper washing.

In Chicago we went to see Esther Larsen; she had also been a missionary. Her family received us royally, while a snowstorm blew outside. It was here that we met and had sweet fellowship with Mary's brother Dave and his new fiancée.

The trip from Chicago to California seemed endless. Since it took several days, we had to stop at a few cabins along the way. We were relieved when we finally reached Manning Avenue in Reedley where Mom and Dad Kroeker lived after moving from Dallas. Only Arthur and Ruth were home when we arrived. The others were married or had jobs in other towns. Dad was especially moved when he saw us. His emotion was particularly noticeable because he was of Victorian stock, and not given to emotional outbursts.

Since Mary's family in Oregon was waiting for us, we hurried on and reached Dallas as the sun was setting. We took a back road to the Smithfield farm where Mary grew up and where most of her family was gathered. Mary's sister and brother-in-law, Anna and Corny, now had little Marciel; her brother Frank and wife Agnes now had a son Eldon and daughter Evelyn; and of course, none of them had yet seen our Buddy. How wonderful it was to be together.

We stayed with Mary's sister and brother-in-law Elizabeth and Sam Reimer. The days flew by too quickly. We had many people to see and acquaintances to renew, but traveling with little Buddy was difficult and Mary needed rest. She took treatments from Dr. Bollman, the family doctor who took special interest in her condition and gave her excellent care.

Knowing that Mary was in good hands, I went on to Klamath Falls to meet my brother Jake and his wife Nada and their little daughter Mary Anne. Then I traveled on to California, making many stops to see friends and relatives.

After a visit in the little town of Parlier, I had a freak car accident at one of the crossroads. Somehow I was pinned under the car. Had it not been for two Christian ladies, the Rickert sisters, who were driving past and stopped to help me, it could have been fatal. They truly did the part of good Samaritans. Living nearby, they took me into their home, got a doctor, and saw to my care. I had difficulty breathing, with a buildup of pain in my side. But a few days later this suddenly cleared up. I was relieved and ready to move on again.

In the meantime I received news that our Buddy was sick with pneumonia—so seriously that it was feared we might lose him. Since Dad Kroeker had planned to go to Oregon to pick up sister Eva and bring her home, he decided to take me along so I could be with Mary and Buddy. By the time I got there, Buddy was much improved, though still weak and fragile.

We decided to return to California where I could hopefully find a job to support my family. But it was the Depression and jobs were scarce. Hearing that prospects were better in Los Angeles, we decided to try there.

We stayed in Garden Grove with our relatives, the John Kliewer family, whose son had married Frieda Neufeld, one of Mary's school friends, and whose other son Otto was now married to our friend Edith. Though grateful for the generous hospitality of this home, we desired a dwelling of our own where we would not be burdensome to friends.

We happened to hear about a growing missionary colony in Glendale and decided to check it out. This colony was actually a little village of small houses, including some "tent houses," which were really little cabins with canvas roofs. They were being put up quickly to provide housing for the many missionaries forced to return from various countries due to the lack of funds from the Depression.

I was offered a job building a foundation for one of these "tent houses," and we were assigned one of the finished "tent houses" to live in ourselves. It was completely furnished with cooking facilities, beds, bedding, and even an icebox. An added mattress was given to us for Buddy, which we shoved under the bed during the day.

It was wonderful to have a home of our own; the fellowship of this "missionary colony" was an extra bonus. We were particularly impressed by our landlady and employer Mrs. Suppes, or *Mother Suppes* as everyone called her. This energetic widow, now in her sixties, together with her helper, also an elderly widow, darted in and out of cabins, arms loaded with linens and bedding. From time to time they'd stop to chat to encourage their missionaries.

The story behind their colony was in itself an example of faith that encouraged struggling missionaries like ourselves. It seemed that Mother Suppes, after the death of her husband, had opened her large home to missionaries passing through. Although the number of missionaries coming home kept growing, her house didn't. Sorrowfully she began turning missionaries away while her heart questioned, "Why should the soldiers of the cross be homeless in their homeland?" Soon she found herself praying, "Lord, if You'll provide, I'll put up some little houses for these missionaries."

She then proceeded to get estimates. The amount needed would be $50,000—an astronomical sum for a widow and for those Depression days.

Some time later a representative from an oil company knocked on her door and asked permission to drill for oil on a little piece of property she owned. "Of course you can," she exclaimed.

Soon oil was flowing and checks were adding up to $10,000, $20,000, and $30,000. When they reached $50,000, she was informed by the company that the well had caved in. There would be no more oil and no more checks. In telling her story, Mother Suppes would add with a wink, "I should have asked for $100,000. My faith was too small. Don't limit God as I did. Ask and expect *big* things."

She continued to challenge her missionaries to "stretching exercises." One of those came our way through our icebox. It was a daily custom in the colony to put out a card requesting ice from the ice man. The cost was a minimal ten cents. Since Mary and I were struggling with our "cash flow," we decided to trim some edges. We would do without the ice for a few days. Mother Suppes happened to pass our "tent house" that day and, noticing the absence of our card, knocked and announced, "You forgot to put out your ice card."

To this we sheepishly answered, "We don't think we can afford it just now."

"What?" exclaimed Mother Suppes emphatically. "Can you not trust God for ten cents? The day might come when you have to trust Him for thousands of dollars. Put out your card immediately."

Mary meekly put the card in the window. It was a profound lesson and Mother Suppes' words would prove prophetic.

We hated to leave the "colony," but Alma Doering wanted me to go on a deputation trip with her car. Our friends Otto and Edith Kliewer insisted that Mary and Buddy stay with them until brother-in-law Art could take them to Reedley.

While there Mary discovered that the railroad offered missionaries half-price tickets, so she boarded a train for Dallas to meet me where I was speaking in churches in the area. Afterwards we went up to British Columbia and visited the family and many churches in that area.

Then, when an invitation came from Christians in Manitoba, from among the Old Order Mennonites whose worship was formal and liturgical, we were somewhat perplexed, wondering what was expected of us.

We simply shared about our conversion and our burden for Africa. To our surprise, they responded with enthusiasm, asking many questions about the Christian life as well as Africa. We stayed several weeks with them, speaking in barns, graneries, and houses, often using the low German, which most understood. Many were saved and some would have gladly accompanied us to Africa. Several farmers shared sacrificially from the fruit of their grain, which touched us deeply. Mutually encouraged, they sent us joyfully on our way.

Coming back to Reedley for Christmas, we had a wonderful holiday season with the family. My brother Arthur gave a plaid blanket to Mary and me and some tinker toys to Buddy. We were touched by these generous gifts on the part of a high school boy. In the days to come we'd treasure the gesture even more and the scene would flash back in our minds, as it would prove to be the last Christmas we shared with him.

26

Pumped Up Shoes...With the Breath of the Spirit

"Once you've got that African wind in your stomach, you'll want to return."
Dallas, Oregon
1938

By God's favor Mary's health was once again restored. Her boils had disappeared and her hair had grown back more beautiful than ever. This was a relief to Mary because some people, now knowing that it had been shaved off in Africa, considered her to be worldly because her "style" appeared to be the popular "bob cut" in vogue at the time. Often she'd hide behind a little felt hat.

Criticism regarding our appearance wasn't the only deflater in our sails. Although we'd been in Africa only two years, we saw everything with different eyes. The carpeting was quite different from the "mother earth" to which we'd adapted, as were the smells, the dress, the language, and the music.

Speaking never came easy for me. The sense of unworthiness, that one with a background such as mine, should address older Christians of spiritual stature and with higher education was overwhelming. Then there was the sense of inadequacy to put in words the quest of my soul while controlling conflicting emotions. How does one describe the joy of seeing a once Satanic worshiper pray to the God of Heaven? How does one express the sorrow of saying "good-bye" to father and mother, perhaps for the last time?

My timid Mary surprised me sometimes with her spontaneity and joyfulness when speaking to groups. Later, when we were alone, I'd question her on this strange phenomenon, to which she'd reply, "The Lord gave me liberty and joy."

In spite of moments of victory, our struggles continued. Kneeling together we'd implore God's grace to communicate our calling with joy and liberty. Now we understood better what we'd read from the biographer of the explorer Henry Stanley and from his own writings:

> "Indeed no African traveler ought to be judged during the first year of his return. His nerves are not uniformly strong; his mind harks back to the strange scenes he has just left and cannot be focused upon that which interests society..."[1]

> "Civilization never looks more lovely when one is surrounded by barbarism, and yet, strange to say, barbarism never look so inviting to me as when I am surrounded by civilization."[2]

1.　　Wasserman, Jakob translated by Eden and Cedar Paul. *Bula Matari*: New York, Liveright Inc.

2.　　Stanley, J. Morton edited by Dorothy Stanley. *Autobiography of J. Morton Stanley*. London, Houghton Mifflin Co.

Such thoughts had, indeed, repeatedly gone through my mind. Sensitivity becomes less acute as time goes on, but those first weeks can be most bewildering.

Then there are decisions to make with well-meaning friends who are not always the best counselors. Again and again we turned to the Lord for guidance. How easy it would be to agree with family and friends who reminded us of the risks to our health, our lack of comforts, the education of our child, or insisting that "we weren't indispensable to God because others could do the job in our place." The temptation to please them, at the cost of our calling, was real. We felt pulled in two directions. In times like those one must never forget that obedience sometimes carries an enormous price, but disobedience is catastrophic.

Before we left Congo the Africans had told us, "You'll be back. Once you have that African wind in your stomach, you'll always want to return."

Now that Mary was back to normal health we were ready to return, and it wasn't just from the African wind. The "breath of the Spirit" had stirred our hearts and was driving our shoes forward.

27

Misplaced Shoes on a Detour

*Belgium tugged on our heartstrings,
but our stay had been but a detour.*

New York—Brussels
1938

Now that our plans were becoming more concrete for our return to Africa, we were getting more anxious to "go home." Yet we cautioned ourselves with Isaiah 52:12: "But you will not leave in haste or go in flight; for the Lord will go before you, the God of Israel will be your rear guard."

We were excited once again to board the freighter *Alex van Opstahll*, which had given us such a pleasant voyage coming the opposite direction. The well-trained crew was commanded by a dedicated captain who had a big black dog. We later heard that this ship was the first one to be sunk in

World War II, and that the captain and his dog stayed on board when it sank in the tradition of sea loyalty.

The ship was scheduled to sail January 20, and we got nervous because the trunk we'd carefully planned and packed hadn't yet arrived from Philadelphia. If it didn't reach the ship by that day, who knows if and when it would follow us on our African safari? On the twentieth we were much relieved to learn that the loading of the cargo hadn't been completed and that departure time had been delayed to the twenty-first. This gave me an opportunity to tease Mary, telling her that the whole ship was waiting for her trunk. However, as the hours passed and the trunk didn't appear, I regretted testing her on such a serious matter. Mary kept watching the shore with anxious eyes. A few hours before the gangplank was to be removed, she pointed and laughed with joy. There was the trunk. God surely had delayed the ship—to test our faith—and to answer our prayer.

The passengers dined with the congenial captain and first mates who were interesting in themselves, and freely shared their knowledge with us novices. There were only seven passengers aboard, all of whom were missionaries. They included Mr. and Mrs. Mosher and their son; Miss Shellenberg, and us. We felt like one big family. Every morning we had devotions together and compared notes on our experiences. We also exchanged unusual recipes, such as making yeast or soap or mayonnaise without oil.

The crossing, however, was rough, so we were glad when we finally had firm soil under our feet. We were greeted by our friends in Antwerp, but this time we couldn't stay with them in their city. In order to improve our French, we needed to be in Brussels, a French-speaking city. It took us just one day to find a small apartment and another day to get installed. The similarities to the apartment we'd occupied previously in Antwerp made us miss the closeness of the friends who'd shared that part of our lives.

Focusing on our goal, we sought counsel from Mr. John Winston, who was one of the administrators of the Belgian Gospel Mission. He suggested that a good way to practice French was to meet with a Belgian couple on a regular basis. At that time most of the students were older and married, so we began to spend time with a couple by the name of Mr. and Mrs. Bauwens.

The Bauwens exemplified patience as they listened to us read and corrected us over and over. Even more valuable than their assistance in the language was their friendship. They had two daughters, Simone and Christiane, who enjoyed playing with our two-year-old Buddy.

I also enrolled at a language school that was called L'Alliance Française. Our budget permitted only one of us to take the course, but I took careful notes so I could share them with Mary in the evenings. With the help of the textbook and my notes, she was able to do the homework and keep up with me. Our professor, Mr. Moutier, was a former bishop of a Catholic mission in China. I found him most interesting and enjoyed the many animated and profound conversations.

Meanwhile, the Bauwens continued to encourage us, inviting us to all the activities. We sat in on the classes at the Bible Institute, assisted at the street meetings, attended services and Bible studies at the B.G.M. churches, the Baptist churches, the Plymouth Brethren churches, and others.

Since we couldn't afford to pay many streetcar fares, we walked long distances on the cobblestone streets. Buddy would sometimes sigh with fatigue. I would try to encourage him by assuring him that all he had to do was put one foot in front of the other.

We developed many friendships, particularly among the students of the Bible Institute. Sometimes we were able to assist them in various ways—one was to give driving lessons to Mr. Jean Knecht, who later pastored one of the larger churches in the town of Liège. Cars weren't plentiful then and many young people in their twenties and thirties had yet to experience their first turn at the wheel.

We enjoyed the Van Steenberg sons, whose father became co-director with Mr. John Winston of the Belgian Gospel Mission. I was impressed as I watched a Belgian and an American working side-by-side in leadership. Later, when war clouds hovered over Belgian skies, Mr. Winston could put the reins in the capable hands of Mr. Van Steenberg.

Quite a few missionaries were coming to Belgium at that time to study the language or to take the tropical medical course in Antwerp. We had good fellowship with many of them and found ourselves going to Antwerp quite often. Here we were allowed to board the ships to chat with the sailors from Congo. This soon developed into regular meetings. Our short African experience had enlarged our understanding and permitted us a greater ease in identifying with them and their needs and struggles.

Since Mrs. Wilson, the manager of the *pension* (boarding house) for missionaries, was ready to retire, a new manager was needed. We began to consider seriously the possibility of staying in Belgium to serve the Congolese on the boats and to care for the missionaries coming in and going out. Beginning at Biola, Belgium had laid a claim on our hearts, with repeated reminders. But a letter from Alma Doering arrived that once more oriented us to Africa. She was planning a tour of all the U.T.M. mission stations and needed a chauffeur. A family, known as the Van Heckens, offered to take on the missionary house in Antwerp. Belgium tugged on heartstrings, but our stay had been but a detour. The final destination was our home in Africa.

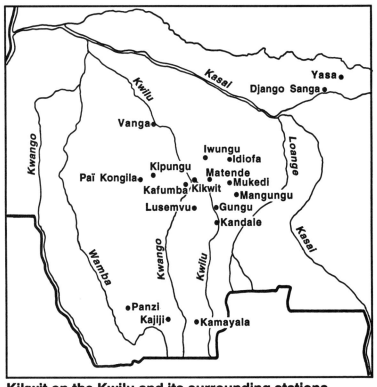

Kikwit on the Kwilu and its surrounding stations

28

Artificial Shoes in Wonderland

Dinner suits were required
to enter the dining room.

The Atlantic Ocean
Antwerp to Matadi
1938

On the fourth of November, 1938, we boarded the SS *Elizabethville*, along with Miss Doering, Miss Dunkelberger, Dr. and Mrs. Laban Smith with their children Junior and Phyllis, Mr. and Mrs. Howard Street, and Miss Birdsell.

The last-minute preparations had been frantic. Several nights I'd worked into the wee hours of the morning on paperwork with Miss Doering and Miss Dunkelberger. Mary had to do the last-minute shopping by herself. This in itself was a major decision-making event as finances were limited and who could tell what possible needs and emergencies might arise the next few years? Mosquito nets and such medicines as quinine were priorities.

Crowds gathered on the first and second floor of the dock to watch the lifting of the gangplank. The chilly November winds blowing against the passengers as they leaned on the rails seemed to match Mary's contrary mood. She was upset because we'd left a pair of scissors with friends in Antwerp who'd promised to sharpen them and bring them to the boat. Now the boat was about to pull out and there was no trace of our friends or the scissors. "How am I going to cut your hair the next four years without scissors?" she sighed. "There's no time to shop now." We rushed around searching every possible meeting place and studying the crowds, but to no avail. The gangplank was pulled away and the ship slid out of the harbor and out to sea.

When the shore became a dot on the horizon, we turned around and started down the stairs toward our cabin. It was then that we realized how weary we both were. There had been so many last minute duties to juggle: keeping track of passports and other documents; making lists of all one's possessions for customs; marking and keeping track of keys for every bag, suitcase, and trunk; sending last-minute telegrams to loved ones; and then dragging baggage on board and up and down stairs.

Looking at Mary's tired face I said, "There's nothing we can do about the scissors now, Mary. We may as well enjoy the trip. Let's take a walk on deck before going down to the cabin." Getting plenty of air, I knew, was necessary in adjusting to high seas, especially for my poor sailor Mary.

Later that evening I noticed that the storm in Mary's heart had calmed. Peeking at her diary I read, "I can't understand why they didn't show up. We need those scissors, but there'll be a way."

This ocean crossing was quite different from our first voyage to Africa. The steamship company offered missionaries first class accommodations for the price of third. We occupied a luxurious cabin and the meals were served with elegance and style; dinner suits were required to enter the dining room. We were grateful for the two white suits a tailor in Belgium had made for me at a reasonable price, and Mary had been able to sew a few more dresses. My favorite was a long waisted cotton dress in soft yellow that made her glow in the candlelight.

Other positive aspects were calm seas and pleasant traveling companions. A Bible study was scheduled every morning, which had to be flexible enough for various interruptions. One of these was the passing of the steamship *Léopoldville*, which was about the same size as ours. (All the steamships bore the names of towns.) Everyone ran for the rails and waved till the ship had passed.

Though the Bible studies were planned primarily for the benefit of the missionaries, others would stop and listen. We particularly noticed a group of priests who began following us every morning up the stairs to the deck, and then settled into chairs nearby. Though they smoked and drank their beer, we knew they were listening. Later when we were invited to hold meetings for workmen on the lower deck, the same group of priests stood nearby and watched. We hoped their hungry hearts were being fed.

Mary took advantage of daily medical classes that a doctor offered. She listened carefully to the lectures on malaria and black water fever and took many notes, knowing how vital the information might prove.

On the ninth of November the boat stopped at Madeira, one of the Canary islands, to pick up coal and supplies. This was a standard stopping place for boats going to Africa and the passengers appreciated the stop since it provided a little change for the long trip.

We were all anxious to go ashore and explore, but when we discovered that a fee was required for landing papers, Mary stoically offered to stay on board with Buddy. Exploring the town and shops I found a little pair of shoes, at reasonable cost, that I hoped would fit Buddy. When I returned with the boots Mary and Buddy were thrilled. "They fit perfectly," Mary exclaimed happily. "They're cute on him, and they'll keep his legs from being bit up by mosquitoes."

But her main consolation came when she saw Miss Doering and Miss Dunkelberger come limping into the dining room, the result of an ox-cart ride. It was all she could do to keep from grinning.

When we got up for breakfast on the eleventh of November, flags were flying all over the ship. It was Armistice Day. A special dinner was planned for that evening, which included several courses of elegant food. I took advantage of the delicate cuisine while Mary nibbled at hers. She still hadn't found her sea legs!

The armistice dinner also marked the time when we were to begin taking quinine. Living in such elegance was like walking in artificial shoes. It was soon to end.

On Sunday, the thirteenth of November, we got up early for a 5 a.m. sunrise service. Sky and ocean glistened so brightly in the morning light that it was almost impossible to tell where they met. At times like that the mystery of God is all-enveloping. How is it possible that mortals may approach the Craftsman of such splendor? Thankfully, it is possible through His Son Jesus. "In Him and through faith in Him we may approach God with freedom and confidence" (Eph. 3:12).

That evening it became our turn to sit at the Captain's table for dinner. The conversation was congenial as the Captain explained we were halfway across the ocean. With a prayer I diverted the conversation to the gospel. I didn't want to risk losing this unique opportunity. The captain listened politely as I laid out the plan of redemption, after which he asked a number of questions. Although he didn't acknowledge acceptance, I believe he had much to ponder on that evening.

For the children's masquerade the following Tuesday, the fifteenth, Mary dressed Buddy like a chief, worthy of his namesake, Chief Kamakashishi. In my opinion he was a little too cute for the honor. I was, however, not a little startled at the ease with which he took on his leadership role. Though it was only make-believe, it seemed to carry a ring of destiny.

On the seventeenth we crossed the equator. This required an initiation ceremony for first-timers. Thus a court was appointed, headed by "King Neptune." This court deliberated on the best way to initiate a first-timer. For some dunking was the chosen procedure; for others a good squirt from a water hose was sufficient. The missionaries were treated quite gently compared to some passengers.

The adult masquerade party followed, which began with dinner and ended 5 a.m. the next morning. While merrymaking and carousing was at its height in the dining room, the missionaries were on the top deck singing hymns of praise to God. The happiest deck, of course, was the upper one, and for these passengers there was no hangover the next day.

The 10 a.m. Bible studies continued as usual and, helped by the approaching African sun, were warming up. As we neared the port, there were frequent discussions among the missionaries about the trip inland. Sometimes the pitch rose to sharper notes. There are many ways to view a mountain and all are valid. There is also a time to unite the various views into one. This is when we must seek the wisdom of God. "The Lord knows the way, and He will guide us," Mary wrote in her diary.

Eventually a decision was reached that we would separate at Matadi. Mary, Buddy, and I would take the train to Songo, the town where Alma Doering's green truck had been sent, drive to Léopoldville to pick up supplies, and then continue to Kikwit where all of us would meet. The rest of the group would go upriver by way of Baningville.

Later, in talking with an officer about the roads inland, he shook his head. "You can expect a difficult trip," he said. "It's a risk I wouldn't be prepared to take." Mary and I looked at each other. It wasn't the first time we'd been discouraged from following God's leading.

On the twenty-first we arrived at Lobito, Angola. It was hot and uncomfortable as we went ashore. When we returned to the boat, Mr. Knight, a local missionary, had come on board to meet with the missionaries. Having just lost his dear wife, his heart was heavy with grief, yet he reported numerous results on the evangelistic efforts in that area. We couldn't help but feel encouraged while we searched our own hearts, knowing that the cost could be as great for each of us.

By mid-afternoon the steamer was approaching the mouth of the Congo River where it would journey upward. Mary and I were getting excited. God had faithfully brought us back to the land of our adoption. We were anxious to move on.

The next day the Congolese crew came on board. Until now, the ship's crew had been Belgian. The new crew put out the anchor and stopped the boat for the evening. A cool breeze was blowing as the sun set over the lush foliage on both banks of the Congo River. Reluctantly we tore ourselves away from the deck and went downstairs for a service with the crew.

We reached Boma early the morning of the twenty-third where most of the missionaries had planned to go ashore to exchange money. We were delighted, as we got off the boat, to be greeted by another local missionary who invited us to come to his house for tea. We followed our guide up a steep hill leading to the Christian Missionary Alliance mission station. The path was bordered by magnificent trees, blooming bushes, and vines—a treat for the eyes. When we reached the house we found an attractive tea with cakes set out on an immaculate tablecloth.

Regretfully we could stay only a short time as we had to be back on board for the processing of legal papers. This was the post where people entering the Congo must register and receive landing cards with the official government signatures. When passing all future government posts, we'd be required to present these cards.

By 3 p.m. we arrived at Matadi where all the passengers disembarked. Beyond that, boats cannot go because of the great impassable Stanley Falls. Mr. Lundt, a missionary with the Swedish mission, was there to meet us. His help with customs formalities and with the baggage was invaluable. After a relaxed meal in his home, Mary and I took Buddy and the Smith children for a walk around the chapel before dropping into bed.

The artificial shoes were left behind. It was time to get out our safari shoes.

29

Safari Shoes—With God at the Wheel

Halfway between...
we got stuck in the sand.
From Matadi to Kikwit
Plus Full Circuit

There was quite a rush the next morning before everyone got away; the sun was already scorching by the time we got on the train. From the experience of our first African train ride, we knew what to expect. Our three-hour ride was enough to make us look like chimney sweeps.

Upon arriving at Songololo, we learned that the truck we were to drive to Kikwit for Miss Dunkelberger hadn't arrived yet. There was nothing we could do but wait. The little train station was run by a Belgian couple, Mr. and Mrs. LaCroix. Although we had never met them before, they received us warmly, taking us to their home and providing water so we could get cleaned up. After this they served us a delicious meal. Here was another opportunity to share the good news we had come to bring to any who would listen—white or black. Their acceptance of the message—and of ourselves— made the stopover an oasis.

The next problem facing us was sleeping arrangements. The Swedish missionaries, hearing of our predicament, came and helped us set up our cots in the train depot. This pampering and kindness, from strangers, could not have been exceeded even had it been a four star hotel. Mary wrote in her diary that evening, "God has His children *partout*" (everywhere).

By 6:30 a.m. the truck had arrived. The clouds and pouring down rain sounded a dismal note as we prepared to begin the next lap of our journey. I was anxious to try out the truck, but on the insistence of our hosts, Mr. and Mrs. LaCroix, I sat down with them and the family to a continental breakfast. Then I went out to start the motor. To my dismay the key Miss Dunkelberger had given didn't fit. Mary jumped up in readiness when I came inside, then stopped short as she noticed my expression. "The key doesn't fit," I said. "We won't be leaving just yet!" We settled back, wondering what we should do. Again there was really nothing we could do but wait and pray. God would have to bring a solution and take over the wheel of this entire trip.

At ten o'clock Mr. LaCroix walked in with an envelope that contained the correct key. Apparently Miss Dunkelberger had realized the mistake and immediately sent the key. I ran out and started the truck. Everyone clapped when the truck purred. We were on our way—with God at the wheel.

Our next stop was Kimpese, which we reached by 3:30. After a short tour of the mission station, we continued to Thysville to the Baptist mission station. Halfway between the two stations, we got stuck in the sand. I let Mary and Buddy out and then set to work with spade and sacks. Before long we were on our way again, arriving at Thysville by about 8:00.

After a night of rest and a short visit with the Caselbows and the Austins, the missionaries who served at that station, we set about getting more food supplies. We also shipped part of our load.

By noon we were once again on our way but had gone only a short distance when a thunderstorm struck. These sudden storms, accompanied with loud thunder and lightning, are common in Zaïre and can be quite frightening. Usually it's safest to wait and proceed cautiously, making sure the roads are passable. Our next stop was Kisantu, which was one of the last places we could get gas and supplies before the road that lay ahead, which was declared *impossible*.

After committing our way to the Lord, we set out about 2:00 p.m. The following night we spent in our car near Kalemvu, a Catholic mission station.

The next morning before we had time for our Psalm of the day and prayer, a young man, who had the oversight of the road, came by and stopped. "Are you needing help?" he asked.

"No," I replied. "We're on a long journey and just stopped for the night. We were about to read a Psalm to start us out. Would you like for me to read it for you?"

"Yes," he replied with eagerness.

After reading the Psalm I asked, "Would you like for me to explain it to you?"

"Yes."

After praying together, we bid our friend and brother "good-bye" and drove on.

Later we stopped to buy some pineapple from some natives, to whom Buddy was a great attraction. The women especially crowded around, pointed, smiled, and made animated comments one to the other. Never before had they seen a little *mountou* (man) with white skin and fair hair.

"Is he a boy?" they asked.

"Yes," we replied.

"Then he's yours. If he were a girl he'd be ours!"

Mary anxiously wrinkled up her brow, but it soon dawned on her that they were paying a compliment. The Africans have their own jargon that often includes proverbs and sayings unknown to the Western mind. In our jargon, they were saying, "Isn't he cute? We're tempted to steal him, but we'll let you keep him." Mary smiled and expressed appreciation for their compliment. Then pointing to their children, she returned compliments in typical mother fashion.

Continuing our journey we crossed the Kwilu River and entered the Kwango, our home district. The sombola in Popakabaka wasn't much of a place—just poles and a roof—but we met a state official who was working there. After visiting with him we gave out the Word to the Africans before continuing our journey.

Darkness had fallen by the time we reached the ferry. Not wanting the family to spend the night by a mosquito and *tsetse*-infested river, I tried to persuade the Africans into giving us a crossing. Reluctantly they agreed. Driving on and off bouncing, swaying planks is risky enough in the daylight, and certainly not recommended for nighttime, so I proceeded cautiously while Mary turned her back.

Upon arriving safely on the other side we congratulated, thanked, and generously rewarded our Africans before continuing to Kenye. There we spent another night in the car. The noises of the darkness and the beady eyes popping out from time to time had kept us awake the previous night, but tonight we gave in to sleep.

Going about our errands in the small town the next day, we met Mr. and Mrs. Lenaerts, a state official and his wife, who invited us for breakfast. Then, after buying gas, we were once again on our journey. Five ferries and 500 kilometers later, we arrived in Kikwit at about 10:00 p.m. We were happy to find the Jantz's still up. What a happy time of reunion followed! To our surprise, we learned that we'd arrived before the other missionaries. Beds were put up for us in the dining room since the guest house was occupied that night by two women missionaries, Kathryn Willems and Anna Enns. We dropped into bed bone weary, but thankful that the trip had gone so well.

The next day we settled into the guest house, also known as the *tin house*. A garage made completely of corrugated tin, it was literally an oven. Fortunately, there were good shade trees around, including a mango tree, piepie trees, and beautiful palm trees. Buddy seemed happy to play in the dirt with the Jantz children, which didn't please Mary too much. Keeping Buddy clean was already a big chore for her. Limited water and scrubbing clothes by hand was a challenge to cleanliness.

Fortunately, an African boy helped Mary the next day; that gave her time to help Fannie Jantz set up beds outside for the group that was due to arrive. My chore was to get some work done on the truck. The springs were hanging low when we arrived and needed to be built up.

By evening of the following day, the expected guests still hadn't arrived. A clap of thunder announced another cloudburst. Everyone ran for the beds and managed to get all the bedding into the house before the sudden downpour. Puffing and panting, Fannie asserted, "We won't set them up again before our guests actually arrive."

Two days later the guests still hadn't come, and fortunately so, for another storm had poured out such torrents that the whole yard turned into a mud hole. I got out and made a ditch to drain some of it off.

The following day was Sunday. Still no guests. Since there was no scheduled church service, we all got in the green truck, which the Jantz children had named *Mosi Manimba*, and drove to Leverville. We had lunch on the way in a shady spot, then continued to the dock to meet Miss Birdsell and the Streets. Afterward we stayed on for a service. Willie spoke in Kikongo and I in English for the Gold

Coast people. When *Mosi Manimba* got her weary passengers back to Kikwit by 8:00 p.m., they were interested only in a little supper and their beds.

Informed by the Streets that Miss Doering and Miss Dunkelberger were in Vanga waiting for me to pick them up, I left early in the morning to pick up my two "D's," as I called them.

It was quite a commotion when everyone got back together at Kikwit. Bodies were running here and there trying to keep their things together. After a big dinner, everyone was ready to retire early.

The next morning in the chaos of getting up and organized, Mr. Eicher, a Swiss missionary from the Balaka mission station, arrived. We were glad to see our dear friend, but had little time to socialize as there were many preparations for the next trip that was planned. Before chauffeuring my two "D's" to Kafumba, I cleaned up our garage home, which was a big relief to Mary. She had been concerned for Buddy's health, and besides, all the belongings of missionaries that were stored there in helter-skelter fashion was depressing her.

From then on, I was to be at the disposal of my two "D's." Our family would be separated for important days, such as Buddy's birthday and Christmas, but we would see each other for brief intervals between various safaris. On Christmas eve Mary wrote in her diary, "It hardly seems like Christmas, but it doesn't need to be the way we feel. The folks at home will be celebrating in a real way, I'm sure." Then later she added, "Didn't know I'd miss him so much."

We were relieved to be together for a short time at the conference at the Shambungu mission station. Here we prayerfully planned the strategy for our coming efforts. It was also a time of spiritual refreshment, mutual encouragement, and personal commitment, on the part of each missionary, for the task ahead.

After the conference Mary stayed on at Shambungu while I continued with the two "D's" on their tour of mission stations. This time I would be away from my family for three months. It was especially hard because there was virtually no means of communication between us during this time.

I learned a lot regarding the layout of the Congo and the missionary activities going on, but it was a tiring trip on roads where one can expect anything to happen, and being responsible for the two ladies who were mission directors.

Mary was happy to be with Elizabeth Lemière again. Many changes had occurred since we'd left her in Africa. She'd married a missionary, Clyde Shannon, and they now had their first baby, Ralph. Before long Mary's nimble fingers were put to work helping Elizabeth sew for her growing family while the two women conversed and got caught up on all the happenings in their separate lives.

Clyde and Elizabeth were busy learning the Chokwe language, the tribal language of that area. We considered it a favored language because the New Testament had already been translated in that dialect. Many more safaris would be required before this could occur for other dialects.

It was a wonderful day when Mary and I were once again reunited. We then proceeded back to Kikwit and then to the Mangungu mission station where there was room for us to stay in one of the houses.

30

Untied Shoes Prepared to Change

Policies would be reviewed
and readapted to the changing scene.

Mangungu
1939

It was too hard for the family to rough it with me in various villages, in primitive quarters, and often in hostile atmospheres. So I usually left Mary and Buddy at Mangungu with the good hospitality practiced at all the mission stations in the area, while I continued to "spy out the land."

The Mangungu mission station was located on the southern edge of the Babunda tribe—a very large tribe that had hardly been evangelized at all. The station was opened by Archie and Ella Haller. They were independent missionaries who adhered to a pattern of mission work different than what was currently being done.

They were seeking to put into practice methods described by Roland Allen in his book *Missionary Methods: Saint Paul's or Ours*, methods that had been successful in China. They carried on no education or medical work; nor did they permit any Bible teaching of any kind on the mission station itself. Their goal was to establish a local church and a school in the village, not on the mission station.

Twenty years or so later this method would have been right on target, but at that pioneer time it had its complications. The Africans did not yet know how to read and were still very much involved in heathen, demonic practices. It seemed to us that they needed the environment of the station to receive the teaching and care they needed.

In spite of our different views, though, we remained the best of friends and maintained high esteem for one another.

Other missionaries at that time felt that mission work should be entirely indigenous. In other words, the life style of the missionaries should be exactly like that of the Africans. They should live in the same type of dwellings, eat the same foods, and so forth. This was commendable, and a policy we would recommend in later years, particularly for Europe, but at that time, it added risks to the already precarious condition of the missionaries. It also contradicted the Belgian administration's policy that required Europeans to keep standards as high as possible in order to bring up the African standard of living.

Many policies in the years to come would be reviewed and readapted to the changing scene. The truths of God's Word are absolute and cannot be altered, whereas the method of our warfare on the forefront of these battlefields must adapt appropriately to world changes. Wisdom to discern how and when to shift with the trends, without compromising truth or sacrificing the heartbeat of the missionary mandate, is the critical issue. Tragic casualties have resulted from wrong decisions at such crossroads.

As we faced our second term we pondered the issue. An indigenous, national church, free from racial or cultural stigma, was certainly the ideal, yet caution flags were waving before our eyes based on our experience from our first term. For one thing, our survival required living conditions different from that of the native people, who had built up their immunity to diseases to which we were susceptible. Another thing we determined to do was distinguish between unique and charming African culture and heathen practices. We'd also concentrate on making disciples and leaders and we'd continue to provide treatment for the sick. Hospitals were few and far apart, and were usually ill-equipped and understaffed. How can we offer healing of the soul while disregarding suffering of the body?

Keeping a balance, we felt was a reasonable goal. This included sanitation, a healthy diet, and avoidance of burnout from overwork. At that time, the process of existing was exhausting. Water for washing bodies and clothes had to be brought—sometimes several miles—from the river. Then, in order for it to be drinkable, water had to be boiled 20 minutes—on an open fire—then filtered and bottled. Washing clothes was another exhausting procedure. Drums of water had to be heated and each piece of clothing rubbed on a washboard. Ironing was performed with an iron filled with hot coals, fired up every so often with vigorous swinging motions.

Food preparation was another challenge. Bread had to be baked from scratch—also on an open fire. Most vegetables had to be grown in the garden, on raised beds, or under shelters of palm leaves over poles and crosspieces. On our periodic trips to the trading post in Kikwit, we'd stock up on staples such as flour, sugar, canned goods, and other items, the variety of which could never be depended upon. Most of the meat on our table came from the chickens we raised ourselves, once in a while from a goat, deer, or pig, which I would butcher and Mary would can or salt, or from dried fish or canned meat such as corned beef. Eggs came from our own chickens or vendors from the village. Purchasing eggs from the latter required a certain ritual. The vendor, usually a man (because women were out working the fields), would arrive with a basket of eggs. Then he and Mary would sit down outside on raffia chairs or bamboo benches and Mary would take one egg at a time and hold it up to the sun. If it had a black spot or appeared cloudy she'd put it aside. In spite of this precaution, we'd often have unpleasant surprises. Sometimes they'd be so rotten they'd actually explode. We learned always to crack an egg in a small bowl before including it in a recipe.

While staying at Mangungu we received a drum of KLIM milk, a well-known brand of powdered milk (milk spelled backward), that was now available at Kikwit. Until that time we had only had canned milk or goat milk, which has a very strong flavor.

To compensate for the efforts in getting such viands was the abundance of tropical fruit: papayas, mangoes, bananas, avocados, lemons, pineapple, guavas, coconuts, and dates.

One of my main concerns was for Mary. How could I keep her from burnout? Teaching had been a calling from childhood, one for which she was particularly gifted. I also knew that the compassionate heart of my *Mama Mbote* would not let her ignore the suffering around her. Then too, there were times when I needed her input and help in areas where her perception and insights were invaluable. She needed to be freed from the weight of the most exhausting and life-threatening duties. For this she must have the help of a *boy*, or a household helper.

We would also maintain certain standards of cleanliness and sanitation. In the tropics hepatitis, infection, and viruses have enormous reproductive powers. We also determined to make our home as cozy as possible. My *Mama Mbote* was a homemaker with an eye for beauty. Throwing a rug on a dirt floor, hanging curtains at the screened windows, placing pictures on the wall, along with situating homemade furniture, made our home, even in the crudest of conditions, a pleasant retreat. Later we'd even ship out our wedding china, which gave added dignity and atmosphere to dinners served to European state officials.

With time, our plumbing included a septic tank, but the water supply was limited to buckets of water. Bathroom fixtures included a homemade cement bathtub, a washstand with an enamel washbowl, and buckets of water.

Although my family was well cared for at Mangungu, we were anxious to be together as a family again. Being without word from one another was trying. When I was finally able to return, our rejoicing knew no bounds. I also was happy to report that I'd found an excellent place for a mission station at a place called *Iwungu Nzamba*. "Someday," I said dreamily, "it will be our home."

31

Walking Shoes With Treasured Moments

Many villages were accessible only on foot.
Vanga
1940

Following my tour of Congo with Miss Doering and Miss Dunkelberger, I was overwhelmed to discover that the large Babunda tribe, east and west of Kafumba, appeared to have no trace of missionary footprints.

At the following U.T.M. conference, I pointed out this fact and was pleased to be given the assignment of establishing a mission station in that tribe.

Facing the task, we were at first confronted by some obstacles. We had hoped to be helped by Miss Thiessen from the Braka mission, but she'd already been requested elsewhere. This meant we'd be entirely on our own.

Single women missionaries were by no means a minority at that time. Someone has said that just as many men hear the call, but their reply is, "Here am I, send my sister." Heaven's books have recorded how much of the advancement of missions has rested on the fragile shoulders of these heroic servants of God. Among them were gifted teachers and skilled medical workers. Some even had mechanical ability. One such industrious woman kept her car in such good repair that she was often called to maintain or fix the cars of others, most frequently those of state officials who would arrive with broken springs.

We were never privileged to benefit from this sister's assistance because, as yet, we didn't own a car. We still had to rely on porters or carriers for our transportation. The *kipoys*—makeshift chairs fasted to a pole on each side and carried by four men—never surpassed walking speed. For someone accustomed to motorcycle-dragging and car-racing, this was quite a test of patience. I dreamed of having a vehicle with a powerful engine. However, had I had the opportunity to sit at the wheel of a high powered jeep with four-wheel drive, I would have completely missed the polishing grace of patience on my walking shoes.

Walking the narrow dusty paths, often with grass high above my head on either side, afforded an opportunity to meditate and pray. Foot travel had the added benefit of keeping me at the level of the Africans. Besides, there were still relatively few roads, so many villages were accessible only on foot.

A greater obstacle was negotiating residence status at Iwungu Nzamba, the village I was convinced God had indicated as His choice and which I'd claimed for Him. Although permission had been granted by the Belgian officials, Chief Kitoko refused to add his signature—in this case a thumb print. Besides his own fears and apprehensions, rumors had reached his ears about the misconduct of Europeans, some of which, regretfully, were true. The interaction of missionaries with neighboring enemy tribes was another source of irritation and contention.

Day after day I sought audience with Chief Kitoko, only to see him look at me over his gourd pipe and shake his head.

Though disappointed, my fascination with these chiefs was growing. They were informed and kept track of every person and every move in the village, yet were unable to write their names or even tell their age. Those were not matters to be concerned about. In estimating my age, they guessed that I must be about 100 years old!

Though only 38, I felt like it was taking a hundred years to get established. Mary also was becoming anxious because the arrival time of our second child was coming due.

Because of the complications we'd had with the birth of our Buddy, we decided, for this child, to take the precaution of being near a doctor. So a couple of weeks before the expected due date, we left for Vanga by boat. On the way we stopped at Leverville. There we sought to encourage the little church with a few meetings and as many visits as time would allow. Then, as we continued down the Kwilu River, I stood beside the captain and engaged in conversation. After the usual course of polite questions I asked him if he knew the one true God. He eyed me with interest, so I continued to tell about Jesus, the Son of God who had come to show us the way to God's beautiful village in Heaven. Without hesitation he embraced the faith, accepting God's Son as his Mediator and Savior. Then, before our astonished eyes, he threw out what Mary called his *Allah paraphernalia,* which was his raffia bag filled with fetishes, charms, and idols. "What a victory over Satan," Mary wrote in her diary that evening.

Weary, but relieved, we arrived at Vanga. There we were welcomed by Dr. Ostraholm and his efficient staff. A house was given to us where we could have privacy and preparations were made for the event.

We will always be grateful to Dr. Ostraholm who stayed by Mary all through the night and, at 7 a.m. of February 15, helped our son Philip Nathan into the world. While Miss Jorgeson, an American missionary, and an African nurse bathed the baby, my heart leaped with thanksgiving for the gift of my olive-skinned son, who bore no resemblance to his fair-skinned Dad.

Our first visitors the next morning were two snakes. Miss Jorgeson yelled and beat at them with a towel until a boy came with a stick. It became exciting for Mary when one of them went clear across her bed. As for our tiny son, while all this rumpus was going on, he peacefully slept in his basket beside his mother. Far more exciting adventures were in store for him in the days to come.

32

Cozy Shoes in a Humble Home

Our hut was by no means a mansion,
but we were cozy and content.
Kangu
1941

Our stay in Vanga was most pleasant. the Ostraholms were an exceptional young couple. The doctor's no-nonsense professionalism was softened by his sympathetic concern and friendliness. Mary and his wife Peggy were soon as close as old friends. Another missionary couple, Mr. and Mrs. Robins, were also stationed there. Their daughter Priscilla was the same age as our Buddy, and the two immediately became playmates.

Before the birth of Philip, we had anticipated having a girl. A name was picked out, and we sometimes referred to our baby as "she," that is, until one evening Mary read the story of Samuel during our time of devotions. Buddy, then six, lifted his reflective eyes and stated, "We can't have a girl yet; first we have to have a little boy, so we can give him back to God." Those words, which somehow carried a prophetic ring, pierced our hearts. We filed them away in the back of our minds, while assuring Buddy that our little girl might indeed turn out to be a boy.

On the morning of Philip's birth our proud Buddy bounced out of the house to announce the big news to his friend Priscilla. "My baby sister's a boy," he hollered.

The entire Ostraholm family was exuberant when they learned that we'd named our son Philip. It was the name they would have chosen had their little Kathy been a boy. Not anticipating other children, they entered the joy of our family, praising God and cuddling Philip as though he were their own. If only one could hold on to happy moments like that. Thankfully they can be stored away, with other treasures, in the bank of cherished memories.

While waiting for Mary to recover I tried to make myself useful. Being informed that the Delco motor, which produced electricity for the hospital, was broken, I worked with Doctor to try to fix it. When we'd repaired everything that seemed to need fixing, we still had periodic shorts. What could possibly be wrong? Finally I noticed a drop of sweat falling from my finger, which was followed by a short. I began to laugh. "Look at our fingers," I said between convulsions, "the sweat dripping from our fingers is falling on the distributor points!"

Another task I took on, which was not particularly one of my skills, was that of "village barber." Both Miss Jorgeson and Doctor fell under my scissors. To my surprise they seemed quite satisfied with their hairstyles that, when considering the latest vogue of African hairdos, were quite acceptable.

Although Mary was well cared for by Miss Jorgeson, who attended her and our baby like a sister, her recovery was retarded by an outburst of the old skin disease. The days stretched into weeks while our food supplies shrank alarmingly. It was a wonderful day when Mary woke up in the morning to announce cheerfully that she felt better than she had for many months. We were able to make preparations for leaving.

I would have liked to take our little family of four *home* to a house of our own, but this was not yet to be. With Mary's health still fragile, I dared not take her to a *sambola*. Thus we returned to Mangungu. The guest house was now full, but our friends gave us a room.

We did our cooking outside. Our kitchen stove was the top of a gasoline drum, balanced on some rocks, with an open fire underneath. Mary caught on to this type of cuisine quite well and managed to whip up interesting meals. She became a pro at fire making and managed to bake our bread over the evenly distributed coals.

Our Buddy found the close quarters of our one room confining, particularly when his daddy was away. He began to weary of hearing, "No, Buddy, don't do that," repeated over and over in the course of a day. Mary was sometimes at a loss as to what to find for him to do. In desperation, one day, she taught him to embroider! Things became more interesting when I started working on the Haller's old truck. Being near daddy and doing like daddy made his day.

After little times of refreshment with the family, I'd tear myself away and start another tour.

Since our return to Africa I'd traveled extensively, first on a tour with Miss Doering and Miss Dunkelberger, and then by myself, when I concentrated most of my efforts on the Babunda tribe. I would go from village to village announcing that a service would be held. In the beginning I needed no loudspeaker. My presence alone stirred up enough curiosity to draw a crowd, and what joy and fulfillment I felt in speaking of what was dear to my heart. At nights, however, concern for my family kept growing until I made the decision that, even though less comfortable, I would take them with me. Later, when I made the proposition, there was unanimous agreement.

So one morning we donned our helmets and set out together. Having the family with me proved to be quite an asset. People in the villages came running just for the chance of seeing this strange little white family. There were, however, some drawbacks. Sometimes I'd interpret an expression of profound interest as a response to the message, only to hear a question such as, "Will you take off your baby's shoes so we can see if his feet are like ours?" The children tired quickly, and for my refined Mary, the crude living conditions made her tasks even more difficult. Thankfully, Setefan, our *boy*, had decided to accompany us. What a wonderful help he was. Yet, as a new mama, there were things only Mary could do. Her diary one evening read, "Though we are appointed to live in tents and *sambolas*, it won't be long now until the Lord will have other things for us." This was typical of my *Mama Mbote* (Mother Star), whom I also called my "upward-looking Mama." She always foresaw a better future. Another evening she wrote, "It's quite a life camping out in the sticks like this, but we are happy in Him. All is well and we can only praise Him."

Upon leaving Mangungu, our first move as a family was to Idiofa. Here I held services that first Sunday, both morning and evening. The next day was wash day. With the help of Setefan carrying buckets of water and rubbing stacks of clothes, the wash was on the line in just a few hours. A short while later Mary went out to check on the clothes and found the lines empty. All the clothes were gone. "Guess your message didn't sink in," she commented. We had to recognize that, to people without clothes, a line full of clean garments waving in the breeze is a tremendous temptation.

We traveled on to Iwungu Nzamba. It was an aesthetic village located on the edge of a cliff in the lush Luano valley. Standing on the edge, we looked over all the surrounding villages and once again claimed the area for God. Selfishly,

Mary and I both saw that, located there, I'd be able to trek around to all the surrounding villages and still be close to home. It became our dream.

Again I tried negotiating with Chief Kitoko. Again he turned a deaf ear, though I noticed the slightest softening in his attitude. He seemed to be starting to enjoy our chats. Still, things didn't seem to be changing. I decided to break off for a while and take the family to Kikwit for a little time of refreshment with our friends the Jantz's. Their open, welcoming arms were in themselves the refreshment we needed. A little while with them put new courage in our hearts and prepared us to face another hurdle.

Upon returning to our *sambola* in Iwungu Nzamba we found that, in our absence, the pigs of the village had chosen it for their residence. Getting them moved out was quite an ordeal. When we did, we noticed bugs and vermin everywhere. In no time our boys' legs were black with vermin.

Hearing that a sanitary agent, Monsieur Dubois, had temporarily settled just outside the village, we asked his advice. He came over with a potent disinfectant that we poured on the dirt floors by the bucketful. We then proceeded to put mats at the windows and a door to keep out all intruders. Privacy from the many faces in the windows was also a relief.

A happy friendship developed with Monsieur Dubois and his wife following this episode. We were thus saddened when we learned that they'd received orders to move on. We invited them over for a last farewell; Mary made a cake on which she wrote *Bon Voyage*. We felt vulnerable as we waved them off. Their nearness had provided a measure of security to our unstable living conditions, and Mary especially would miss their friendship.

While staying in the *sambola* at Iwungu Nzamba, Chief Katchunga, from the little village of Kangu nearby, came to see us and invited us to take residence in his village. At the time we knew nothing about Kangu. From my previous visits there it had appeared to be a friendly village. It also seemed like a defeat to accept this compromise, but it was time for the family to put down some roots. Besides, I reasoned, Chief Kitoko might still change his mind. I'd arrange to visit him often.

In spite of the fact that Chief Katchunga had made the offer himself, it would take another month before the agreement was finalized. I showed my gratefulness with the gift of a blanket that, in his eyes, was of great value. It not only provided warmth at night, but when worn over the shoulder, added distinction and recognition.

Chief Katchunga had given us permission to establish a *chapelle-école* (Chapel School), a structure that would serve as church and school. But the first thing to go up was a little hut. It had only enough room for a homemade table of bamboo poles across one end, which served for storing and preparing food, and a sleeping room for Mary and the two boys. In order to stretch out completely, I found it necessary to set up a tent under a tree right next to the hut. Our hut was by no means a mansion, but we were cozy and content all together as a family of four.

We soon had many callers, including the elder, or judge of the village, and his eight wives. Two of his sons, Bumbe and Kalerki, were among the first to respond to the gospel. With their background, however, and being illiterate, their spiritual growth would be slow and painful. It was necessary to make petition at God's mercy seat for more grace, patience, and wisdom to interpret truths in a way they could understand, and for constantly repeating them.

Another daily caller was a hen I'd purchased from other visitors. Every day she came in and laid one egg under the table. This continued until there were 13 eggs. In the course of time mother hen proudly marched through our bamboo door, followed by all her 13 chicks.

33

Light Shoes...in a Dark Night

Light from our window was the only light around.
Kangu
1941

The building of our *chapelle-école* didn't go as fast as anticipated due to the difficulty of finding reliable workmen. Their value system put earning wages low on their priority list. Men would offer their services, but after working a day, they'd disappear in the forest to hunt and drink, and fail to show up for several days. When they did return, they usually had hangovers and were preoccupied over their palavers, mostly over women. Work schedules and time budgeting were unknown disciplines.

So it was with a sigh of relief that we put our finishing touches on our *chapelle-école*. The walls were made of poles with the spaces and cracks between filled in with mud. The roof was made of grass. On one side there was a veranda enclosed with bamboo, which was to protect the mud walls from being destroyed by the rain. One half of this veranda was used for storage, and the other for a prayer room. On the opposite side of the *chapelle-école* was a room that we called our apartment. Next to our apartment there was another veranda that we used as our dining room.

Since there are no taboos against staring and gawking, and since we were the main subject of gossip and discussion in the village, mealtime on our veranda was a spectacle not to be missed. Never had they seen people use knife or fork and they were fascinated over the strange bricks we called bread. I decided it was time to end the circus performances by enclosing the veranda with a mud wall, and to do it before the arrival of the state official and his wife who had accepted our dinner invitation. When the work was finished we found the new room a little dark, but what a relief to eat alone. The luxury proved to be short-lived, however, and would not serve to impress our expected guests because, just before the state official was due to arrive, our mud wall was swept out by a bad storm.

It took courage to try again, but this time we put bamboo on each side of the mud wall. After laying down bamboo mats, the preferred task of our workmen, and installing the table and chairs I'd built at Mangungu, the room took on the appearance of a dining room. For the *chapelle-école* I made bamboo benches and a pulpit. We'd managed to acquire a good number of slates at Kikwit, which served as miniature desks and scratch paper. Mary made her own blackboard with a piece of cloth; then, with Buddy's crayons, she traced the letters of the alphabet, vowels, and syllables her students could copy on their slates.

The schoolboys, most of whom were teenagers and adult men, were as irregular as the workmen. There just didn't seem to be much incentive for learning. Only a few applied themselves enough to read and write.

While Mary taught reading and writing, I taught simple songs, some that I'd learned at Kafumba, and some I'd translated myself. These they easily adapted to their own lively rhythm, and I soon found I had their full attention. Singing was definitely more popular than reading. Taking great pains, I'd explain the songs in the hopes that they'd understand the message. One song, whose rhythm they enjoyed particularly, was also a Bible verse that I so wanted them to comprehend.

> "Behold, behold, I stand at the door and
> knock, knock, knock,
> (Here I added emphasis by pounding the bam-
> boo bench, which made quite a hollow noise.)
> Behold, behold, I stand at the door and
> knock, knock, knock.
> (More pounding)
> If any man hear my voice,
> (Hands around mouth)
> If any man hear my voice,
> And will open, open, open the door,
> (With arms outstretched)
> I will come in.
> (Hands toward heart)"

I could tell by their blank looks that I just hadn't gotten through. Stopping to analyze it, I remembered that, in fact, they didn't have doors. Openings to their huts were a couple of feet off the ground to keep out animals and fowl. Over these were pieces of bamboo tied together, which were then slid in place or fastened for night. During the day the *openings* were always open. Then too, one never knocks when desiring to enter a home. One stands and coughs!

A song that adapted more easily to their culture was, "The Light of the World Is Jesus." Light was a valuable commodity as most had no flashlights, lanterns, or kerosene lamps. Darkness emphasized the fear of evil spirits and other terrors. The light from kerosene lamps shining from our window at night was the only light around. With the basis of our little light shining in the eerie night, I could easily illustrate:

"The whole world was lost in the darkness of sin,
The light of the world is Jesus."

This song quickly became a favorite. How we loved to hear them sing it with gusto and understanding.

Meanwhile Mary, persevering with her vowels and sounds, was apparently having competition. Disturbing noises were coming out of the walls. What could they be? Picking around in the mud of one wall I discovered that the competition was from a chorus of numerous frogs—the one creature most Africans feared far more than snakes because they are renowned for incarnating the spirits of dead relatives. It became necessary to close the school to have a "take the frogs from the walls" day. I had hoped to have some help in pulling the creatures out, but not a soul showed up to lend a hand or to witness this procedure. When they were all collected in buckets, we numbered 40 large frogs. Apparently they'd come up from the ground, dug holes in the mud wall, and taken residence. It was a problem never repeated in our missionary career, for which we were grateful.

After we were rid of the frogs, the schoolboys helped to repair the walls, which we then whitewashed. Mary saw to it that we got our little apartment whitewashed at the same time. A short while later she had cheery curtains at our one window, which created a homey atmosphere.

After this interruption everyone seemed a little more ready to buckle down to schoolwork, though Mary had now resorted to a gimmick. She offered to provide a pair of shorts as a reward to any student who achieved regular attendance through a school term. Then, to make the incentive hotter, she offered remuneration for odd chores in the way of a white shirt to go with the shorts. This meant a lot of extra work for Mary.

At Kikwit we were able to obtain bolts of denim and unbleached muslin, which she cut *en série*, then spent hours stooped over her little hand-operated sewing machine. Without a doubt, she carried the heaviest part of the bargain. I was not surprised, when we had an awards ceremony conferring recognition on those who had put out a little effort, that Mary beamed the brightest throughout the delight, cheers, and enthusiastic clapping.

34

Heavy Shoes in Black and White

Loneliness, even greater than fear,
was a constant struggle.

Kangu
1941

We were learning many things about Kangu that had been hidden from our eyes when negotiating with the chiefs. The ferryman on the Kwilu River refused to take us across when he found out that we were going to locate in that fearful village reputed for its crime and witchcraft. This was alarming news for me because it affected the safety of my family, so often alone, since I traveled for days at a time in the surrounding villages. The profession of a pioneer missionary isn't reduced to a nine-to-five job. Foot travel didn't permit me to make it home every evening, and it was late into the night when, seated around a fire, I'd have those talks that explored and often exposed the depths of hearts.

Besides the dangers of the power of darkness, including the superstitions, the taboos, the curses, the fetishes, and the fearful power of *Manganga*, the witch doctor, there were physical dangers. As I traveled, my rifle was always in proximity in case an animal or snake darted across the path. Mary and the children, on the edge of the village, were not in the most sheltered place.

Communication between Mary and me had to be transmitted by couriers, some of whom were irregular. There was no access to the village of Kangu by road, so no vehicles could reach her. If anything happened to my dear ones, it would take several days for me even to know about it. What would I do if I came home to a tragedy? Committing to God the safety of what was most precious to me became a daily struggle, requiring daily surrender. Oh, how I missed them. Had I not the support of Mary's missionary heart and God's abundant grace, I could not have stood it.

I remembered how Dr. Pettingale used to challenge his students training for missionary service. "You can expect to go *by faith plus nothing*," he'd say. In those years, before missions were organized with programs, policies, and orientation, faith was the main criteria for all potential missionaries. Now, in the interior of Africa, either alone on the trail or with a group of ten or more carriers, all of whom were bound by superstition, I found myself adapting the statement to, "The only way to advance is *faith plus God*." When He says "Go," He also says "Lo"—"Lo, I am with you always."

I had employed a night watchman, but these men were known for sleeping on the job. Some had even been known to sleep so soundly that they hadn't even wakened when mice chewed on their toes. While the state officials had their policemen to guard them and their families, I had to entrust Mary to the protection of angels and to the One who promised, "I am with you always."

I was thankful that Setefan, our house boy with whom mutual attachment and trust was growing, was with Mary during the day. I was also glad that our Buddy, like a little man, frequently had words of reassurance for Mary when he noticed she was anxious or upset. Yet, there were times when I was put on alert.

One day our mail carrier from the village who'd been trekking to the trading post of Idiofa to pick up and bring back our mail, suddenly announced he was quitting. "Why?" I wanted to know.

"There was blood on the path," he replied.

"So what did you do?" I asked.

"I followed the trail of blood to the bodies of two men. They were traders on their way to Idiofa to sell their cloth [woven mats from raffia used as tender]. I'm afraid the murderers have already been to the witch doctor to ask him to cast a spell on the first person who reports this," he explained. "Also, I don't want to be suspected by those who know that I use that path."

So we lost a good mail carrier, and it was very hard to get another. In fact, we never again had a reliable mail carrier from the village of Kangu.

Later when an administrator came to investigate the murder, four men were arrested. Two of them had been working with us. Had they investigated further, more crimes would have been disclosed.

Mary dreaded the times of separation. Loneliness, even greater than fear, was a constant struggle. She tried to be brave and face the inevitable, but one day she reminded me that it had been a year since she'd seen another white face. Knowing her love of people, I could understand the dreariness and ache of her heart, even though she had her children.

It wasn't just another white face that she longed for, but another Christian brother or sister, black or white, who could share on an adult and spiritual level. She longed to compare recipes, talk about clothes, confide in another mother her excitement over her baby's first tooth, first words, or first steps, or ask advice about discipline or health

problems. There were times when she felt the need of someone who could help her deal with rebellious or distracted
workmen or someone nearby at night when eerie sounds
filled the air.

On rare occasions we'd have the visit of European traders or state officials. Some were of the scoffing kind, frankly
expressing that they thought we were stupid for wasting our
lives in such a desert when there weren't even financial
benefits.

From time to time we'd return their visits. One time it
was our turn to question sanity. A couple had a chimpanzee
named Katrina who had a nasty disposition and who obviously couldn't be trusted. When we came anywhere near her
proximity, she'd throw sticks and sand at us. It seemed to
add a visual dimension to the unseen battle we knew was raging between the forces of evil and righteousness.

At one of my trips to the trading post to get mail and supplies, the woman at the post office asked if I wanted a dog. I
looked with amusement at the mutt that had some resemblance to a collie, and seemed to have similarity in character. After petting the little animal and playing with him a
little, I told the woman that I'd be pleased to accept. It was
exciting to come home with the dog, knowing it would liven
up the dreariness of my family and, hopefully, provide
added protection.

The family, of course, was delighted. We called him
"Black and White" because his fur was black and white and
because it seemed to us that everything around us was either
black or white. The Africans didn't even seem to have words
for other colors in their dialect except yellowish gold. Where
the plains were concerned, and even the villages, they didn't
need any other words. Raffia was used for clothing, and even
their art was in these basic colors. We would, of course, learn
to appreciate these colors, and Africa certainly has many
splendid colors in foliage, flowers, birds, and dress, but just
there and then, color seemed to be absent.

Black and White was a wonderful dog. He received ample affection from my family and the Africans, which he also reciprocated. Since we didn't yet have a door to our little apartment, we tied him to a pole near the entrance at night. This seemed to work out well until one night the jackals came and fought with him. The poor little dog was no match for the jackals, so he suffered considerable injury. Not realizing that jackals are carriers of rabies, we didn't get unduly excited until we saw men coming to us, one carrying a chicken over a pole, and another carrying Black and White, who was barking furiously. "Black and White killed this chicken in a nearby village," they sadly announced. The poor dog died soon after, still barking furiously.

"*Nzambe ikele!*" (God is!) said the Africans standing around. It was the comment made by Africans at unexplainable circumstances. Mary and I found it quite suitable. Then, while singing woeful songs, they buried Black and White.

As spectators to this scene, we wondered at God's care and protection. How could it be that with all the handling of the dog, no one was bitten?

My next concern was for the family. Buddy was standing by with tears on his face. His little companion was gone. I knew my family would now be lonelier than ever during my absence. It was evidenced, a short time later, by a poem Mary penned in her diary while alone in our little grass apartment:

Being a Missionary

Out where the loneliness presses around me,
Looking on sights that are sordid and dreer.
Strangely abiding—yet surely God called me.
Why do I wonder if Jesus is near?
Strangeness of living—strangeness of people,
Have I not come with a gospel of cheer?
Why is my heart then depressed with its
    burdens?

Isn't my comrade—My Jesus—out here?
God, teach me quickly to do without
    friendship,
How to let go of those things that are dear
—How to be rid of this self that is binding me
—Surely My Master—My Jesus— is here.

He, who was God, took the form of a servant,
Humbled Himself unto death, without fear;
Lonely, forsaken, despised, and rejected,
My Blessed Savior—My Jesus—came here.
Father, forgive me my failure in serving
—Heartache, depression, regrets disappear!
Born of the cross a new courage infills me;
Jesus—My Victory—My Life—is here.

35

Bright Sandals in Colors of Faith

She feared that some of the fetishes
and tales might incite curiosity.

Kangu
1941

As I watched my two children grow in the bush I became concerned by the fact that they had no Christian playmates. Another concern was my observation that Buddy was dragging his feet in schoolwork. What bothered Mary the most was the influence our wicked surroundings could have on him. She feared that some of the fetishes and tales might incite curiosity, cause him to accept the fetishes as toys, and open the door for occult meddling. Mary expressed this concern in her diary with this statement: "Buddy is spending far too much time with the natives and I don't like it at all."

For one thing I could be thankful, and that was the fact that most of their time was spent with their mother, who was taking motherhood seriously. Another poem found its way into her diary.

> While she darns her children's socks,
> She prays for little stumbling feet;
> Each folded pair within its box
> Fits faith's bright sandals, sure and bright.
> While washing out with Mother pains
> Small dusty suits and frocks and slips.
> She prays that God may cleanse the stains
> From little hearts and hands and lips.
> And when she breaks the fragrant bread,
> Or pours each portion in its cup
> For grace to keep their spirits fed.

No doubt Mary had ample opportunity to pray such prayers since much of her time was spent "washing out with Mother pains" our very dirty clothes. Her machine was a washboard I had made; her soap she either made herself or was the strong-smelling palm oil soap I sometimes purchased; and her energy was produced by her own two hands. By this time Setefan was married and had a child of his own, so he was no longer our boy.

Keeping a toddler clean on dirt floors was a major frustration. "Philip has been swimming in the dirt today; I had such a hard time keeping him clean," was a concern she stated frequently, as well as, "You can't guess what Philip had in his mouth today." Her eyes continually scanned the floor—and her baby—for traces of bugs or scorpions.

Then there was the nightly ritual of foot inspection to detect the invasion of jiggers. These are tiny ticks that burrow into the skin and rapidly hatch larva. Many of these inspections resulted in a removal operation with the use of a sharp, disinfected needle. The children considered jigger extraction to be minor surgery, especially when it involved a bundle or a "nest" of jiggers. When I was home I took over this procedure, but when I was gone, Mary battled the kicking and screaming alone.

After the jigger ritual, we had our family devotions—a soothing time that also brought us close together. We were grateful for the books we'd brought along, such as *Egemmeier's* and *Hurlburt's Bible Story* books, which we read from cover to cover. The children would then pray in turn, using their own words.

Once tucked in their beds, we'd stay with them till they were asleep. It was one way we could contribute to their sense of security. Buddy still slept on a camp cot as he had ever since our return to Africa. Philip slept in a crib I'd built especially for him when he outgrew his basket. Actually, it was a cage enclosed with a screen to protect him from snakes, bugs, mosquitoes, and especially the tsetse flies. It had a door that opened to permit him to get in and out, and enabled Mary to pat his back and pull up his covers. It also folded down, so it traveled with us everywhere we went.

Buddy's cot was placed under our one and only window until one night, during my absence, he was awakened when he heard something at the window that frightened him terribly. Mary picked him up and brought him to her bed. From then on, every time I was away, he slept in our bed. It was a big metal bed I'd purchased from Mangungu missionaries returning to America. Prior to this, we too had slept on camp cots.

From the same returning missionaries, we'd also acquired a cookstove that facilitated the cooking ritual for Mary. She could now bake her bread in a real oven instead of in a kettle nestled in live coals.

Another challenge to cooking was finding food. The nearest store was a distance of two days of foot travel. The canned vegetables, meat, and sardines that we obtained there were carefully rationed. She thus had to supplement our meals from a garden of her own.

My dad kept us supplied with seeds he enclosed with his letters, but the soil was sandy and the water, which had to be carried up from the river, depended on either the unpredictable water carriers or ourselves. I was able to bring in better soil from the forest, but watering was a constant problem. We did manage, however, to have a few good crops of tomatoes, peppers, squash, beans, and especially eggplant, which when ground, made excellent baby food.

From the village we were able to obtain sweet potatoes, corn, and manioc. The manioc leaves served as spinach and the roots as potatoes. People passing through from time to time brought us such fruit as grapefruit, pineapple, bananas, guavas, and papayas. To supplement our meat supply, we raised chickens and purchased whenever possible a pig or a goat that I would butcher and Mary would then can.

On one occasion we bought a young pig and put him in the care of Atlabwe, who promised to fatten him up so he'd be fit for butchering. We trusted Atlabwe because he was a *mbutu* or elder of the village of Bilumba.

One Sunday, however, Atlabwe came to Kangu and after the morning service was conversing with me when he added nonchalantly, "The pig doesn't eat anymore."

"What's wrong with him?" I asked.

"He died."

When this was repeated in the village, I learned that no one believed Atlabwe had spoken the truth. "Why?" I asked.

"Because no one tells the truth about such things."

I realized that I would just have to accept the fact that here, as anywhere, dishonesty is part of human nature.

A week later, however, I was to be much more amazed. Following a service in his town of Bilumba, Atlabwe confessed that he had sold the pig. A tiny seed of truth had penetrated his hard heart and had begun to sprout.

Mary burst into joyful laughter when I reported this to her. While I'd been trekking in the villages, she'd been faithful washing and mending little socks to "fit faith's sandals, sure and bright." Sharing the blessings made it all seem worthwhile.

36

Garden Shoes
Sowing and Reaping

At one meeting even the
witch doctor showed up.

Kangu
1941

Although I'd conducted services in Kangu prior to our establishing residence there, our first Sunday morning after our move was blessed by a good attendance. The people sat under large, beautiful palm trees as I spoke about the healing of the man of Bethesda, explaining that disease is a picture of sin that only Jesus can heal.

Many services followed in the village itself and some by our little hut. At one meeting even the witch doctor showed up. Though we wondered at his motives, we were glad to see him.

One thing about communicating with primitive tribes is their childlike frankness. We welcomed questions or remarks hoping, of course, to use them as springboards for further discussion, clarification, or understanding on our part. At times there was little response, if any. We wondered if anything was getting through at all. The messages that held the most interest were those that touched on sorcery and witchcraft.

One Sunday morning in Iwungu Nzamba, using their hostility to other tribes as a basis, I gave a message on the fall of man and his enmity with God. Then I showed how reconciliation was possible through the blood of Jesus, and how that could bring friendship with God and hope of eternal life. A woman with a child at her breast lamented loudly, "If my mother had only known that before she died." They all knew there was life after death and that it had to be a better place. The question was how to get there.

In another village as I was speaking about Jesus—how He walked the same dusty paths, and how He reached out and touched the blind man or took the hand of a dead girl—a woman exclaimed, "I always knew there was someone like that, but I didn't know His name!"

When I was away Mary would hold the service. At one time she told about the sufferings of Jesus which the Spirit used to stir hearts. Another time, after a death in the village, she spoke on death, the consequences of sin, and about the hope of resurrection. She wrote in her diary that evening, "The Lord was near and gave listening ears as His Word was read."

Every time I'd return from trekking in the villages she was anxious to hear my report on how the message had been received or, as she put it, "to share the spoils."

Meanwhile there were more stories of crime and sorcery in the village. We wondered how we had ever dared to settle in Kangu. One day I invited Chief Kitoko and the other under *kapitas* or chiefs of Iwungu Nzamba to Kangu. In the course of our visit I explained the salvation that was provided by "the big chief in Heaven." They showed much interest and even made a verbal acceptance, but we wondered if they really understood. With their background we knew we'd have to let time prove if the profession had been real or just to please us. Their lives would show if they had actually broken from the bondage of their past.

We had similar talks with Chief Nkesa of the village of Ibwiti, and Oyom, chief of Bilumbu, after his release from prison. We continued to sow the "seeds of the Word" in Kangu and the surrounding villages of Ibwiti, Imbono, Impkni, Iyassa, Bilumbu, Idiofa, Pomongo, Iwungu, and others. Then, as we watered the hard ground with prayer, waited, and hoped, the first sprouts appeared. On February 16, 1941, several confessed Christ.

For fear that they might confuse salvation with baptism, we proceeded reluctantly and carefully with baptism. But on April 6, though there was only one candidate, we witnessed this memorable and blessed event. Listening to the testimony of this candidate, a son of an elder in the village, brought tears of joy.

It wasn't till September 7 that another baptism took place. This time there were four candidates: Makwenge, Mbumbi, (another elder's son), Kalerki, and our Buddy. Our hearts thrilled in the morning as we listened to their testimonies and at 3:30 we proceeded to the water's edge where they expressed obedience to Christ and confirmed that they had chosen death of the old life of sin, and resurrection through new life in Christ. The communion service that followed resounded with songs of thanksgiving and praise.

37

Eager Shoes and Spinning Wheels

The greatest strides...have been
made one footprint at a time.

Panzi
1941

Trekking from village to village continued, sometimes on
tiny winding paths, often uphill, and sometimes down into
the valleys. In the morning the paths were wet and muddy;
in the afternoon and in the evening, dusty. I regretted that
footwashing was not an African custom. I encouraged myself
that I wasn't the first missionary to spend time on the trails.
From the footprints of Jesus to the apostle Paul, and down
through the centuries to pioneers such as David Livingstone,
the greatest strides of missionary advance made have been
one footprint at a time.

In spite of this knowledge, Mary and I found ourselves praying for wheels. In order to bring supplies from the trading post at Kikwit I had to hire porters. The time and effort for that seemed a waste. Every time I went to Kikwit I checked the vehicles for sale in the hopes of finding something within the means of our small savings, but nothing came into view.

Meanwhile, war was raging full blast in Europe. This promoted the popularity of radios, even in places like Kikwit, because people wanted to keep abreast of the war. We learned that Belgium was now under enemy occupation, and we wondered about our friends. Germans living in Congo were being taken prisoner, as were Italians. One of our U.T.M. missionaries, Mr. Baiotti, of Italian nationality, was arrested. We tried on various occasions to encourage his Swiss wife.

While industries were crippled and supplies cut off in some parts of the world, industry in the Congo began to pick up. The palm oil was needed for primer paint on airplanes; rubber was also in great demand. Thus the oil companies were making good profits. The boats that transported the palm oil and rubber to America then came back with American goods. At that time all the American brands of foods and specialties were available for company workers—and even missionaries—if they could afford them.

The companies began to purchase newer cars and trucks and to sell their old ones at giveaway prices. So it happened that on one of my trips to Kikwit I was able to purchase a 1933 Chevy truck for a song. It had, of course, many problems in which repair and parts were required. On a subsequent trip to Kikwit, I found a similar truck with worn-out parts different from those of the first. Eventually, when the two trucks were combined and after a coat of paint, we ended up with a fairly good baby.

In the meantime, we hobbled along on dusty roads with the better of the two while the old engine puffed and panted. It also required gas that our pocketbook often couldn't afford.

On the agenda was a conference at Panzi that we so wanted to attend, but counting our francs, there was no way we could purchase sufficient gas for the journey. When our Swiss missionary friends, the Eichers, offered to meet us in Kikwit and let us ride with them to Panzi, we gladly accepted. In the meantime, however, they'd had a change of plans that they were unable to communicate to us.

We waited in Kikwit until the day before the conference was to begin. Buddy sat on a gatepost in front of the mission house, waiting to announce to us that the pickup was arriving. But the pickup never came.

Mary and I were adjusting our thinking to the probability that we would not get to the conference, but noticing Buddy's anxious face, I set my mind to finding a solution. With a prayer in my heart I approached the merchants at the Compagnie Kasai, where we purchased our supplies, and asked if they had merchandise that needed transporting to Kahemba (another large trading post near Panzi).

"You've come at just the right time," they responded. "We have a load of *makayaba* (dried fish) that needs transport to Kahemba, and at the same time you can take the mail." The remuneration they offered us was abundantly adequate for the gasoline needed.

Mary was overjoyed when I brought this new report. Though she'd hesitated to mention it, she had felt sure that it was God's plan for us to be at this conference. Her diary carried a triumphant annotation: "The devil sure got licked today. We'll be going to the conference after all."

We left early the next morning, hoping to reach the mission station at Kandale for night. When we arrived there, we found that the missionaries had already left. So we decided to continue our journey to Kahemba. This meant going through the plains by night. At that time it was considered a dangerous journey. Buffaloes were plentiful, as were lions and leopards. It also involved going through several tribes. Though somewhat uneasy about this, we weren't nearly afraid as the two African boys we had along. They hugged each other as they rode in the back of the truck. Later we learned that these tribes were on friendly terms. It was the people from Kangu who were the tribe considered to be most feared!

We arrived in Kahemba with the first rays of dawn. Early mass was being held at the Catholic church, but the Portuguese, the people we had to deal with, were not attending. They were happy to see us—and especially their mail—which, coming with us, had arrived several days earlier than expected. They showed their appreciation by cooking us a delicious breakfast that included four eggs each.

After unloading our smelly shipment of fish we continued our journey to Panzi, arriving amidst cheers of surprise. Everyone had given up seeing the Kroekers. The missionaries from Panzi were also pleased to have their mail delivered personally. Our Buddy was happy to find himself surrounded by playmates.

Because of lack of space, Mary was asked to set up her camp cot and Philip's crib with some ladies, while I set up Buddy's cot and mine with some men. This didn't bother Mary at all. She and Mrs. Peters, who also had a baby, talked like teenagers most of the night.

The first meeting of the conference was open to missionaries and Africans alike. It was preceded by a barbecue, African fashion. Corn, still in their husks and with outer leaves, were roasted on a large bonfire. That evening their African evangelist Petelo (Peter), who also presided at the meetings, asked me to speak. I accepted, though I would rather have heard him.

Petelo at Panzi was like Timothy at Kafumba—humble, hard-working, and trustworthy. Much of the fruit at Panzi was the result of the patient, persistent work of Petelo. Later I had the opportunity to request his help at Kangu, which he graciously gave. We'd learn that not only was he a gifted speaker, but he also had a wealth of illustrations from African customs, particularly about animals, that he used skillfully. He was also fearless of the people of Kangu. This surprised everyone, since he was from another tribe and was fully aware of the reputation of Kangu. We felt small before this brother.

The conference was a time of refreshment for us all. Many had come with heavy hearts, burdened with disappointment and discouragement. Gathered together in fellowship, spirits began to lift.

I was asked to give the message for the last evening. The topic I chose was "The Day of the Feast," based on John 7:37-39, when Jesus, *on the last day of the feast*, invited the thirsty to come to Him. There He promised that, out of them and through the Spirit, streams of living waters would pour forth.

The Spirit of God used His Word that evening. Missionary after missionary told of battles they'd faced that had been so fierce they'd been tempted to give up. Together we reaffirmed commitment and claimed the power of the Spirit to go out and pick up our weapons once more.

After the conference, we went to see the new mission station at Kajiji, which was an outpost of the Shambungu mission station. The Zooks and the Smiths were establishing it there, to be later joined by the Shannons. A beautiful location, it was rightfully named *Belle Vue* (Beautiful View).

The evening before we were to leave, our friends made a special birthday dinner for Mary. Knowing how lonely she'd been over the past year, I was pleased that she could celebrate in the warmth of friendship.

We had thought to leave early in the morning, but decided that the heat was more to be feared than the dangers of darkness. We chose, once again, to cross the plains by dark.

Reluctantly we said good-bye to our friends and started our journey, trying to reach the ferry before nightfall. The fragrance of their fellowship followed us a long distance. It delighted us later, as we sat waiting for our ferry, to see Buddy enjoying the picnic lunch they'd sent along.

We reached Kandale by 5:00 a.m. After a little rest, we continued our journey, arriving at Kikwit completely exhausted by 5:00 p.m. The family was bothered by the heat in Kikwit, and especially Mary as she cooked dinner by an open fire. The Jantz's had not yet returned.

I decided to take advantage of our being in the proximity of Leverville to pay a visit there. I was anxious to know how the little church was progressing. Buddy and I set out to catch the boat, but were disappointed to see it pull out just as we reached the dock. The next day we made it to the shore in good time, and at Leverville we found the little church steadily growing. Mary was encouraged, a few days later, when we returned with the good report.

In the meantime, word had come from Kajiji requesting that I bring a load of building supplies from Kikwit. This time I set out alone. The Jantz's had returned, and I felt the family would be more comfortable staying put.

Once back in Kikwit, the assignment completed, Mary and I realized that it had been a month since we'd left Kangu. It was time to get back, and we felt ready. By this time, however, the truck was travel weary and seemed to be just limping along. Every time we reached a hill, Mary and the boys had to get out and walk while the poor old truck groaned and agonized its way to the top.

It was dark by the time we reached Kangu. We walked into our little house that looked more like a storeroom than a home, and were pleased to find our beds still there waiting for us. It was time to give our bodies and our poor old truck a good rest.

38

Army Boots
on Crippled Feet

Buddy…came to her bedside and
commanded, "Mother, rise up…and walk."

Kangu
1941

After a month's absence there was much to be done to
get our little house livable again. Before leaving for conference, Mary had washed and put away curtains and bed-
spreads, and packed up all our belongings to protect them
from driver ants and other four-legged thieves.

Driver ants were exceptionally large ants equipped with
knifelike pinchers; they were capable of devouring everything in their path. They march in perfect formation, like
soldiers going to war, and their approach is announced by a
loud rumbling sound. The best way to combat this army is by
a fast retreat.

Considering the reputation of our location, we were pleasantly surprised to find that our trunks and belongings were still where we had left them. That in itself was reassuring and confirmed that we had gained a measure of respect. We would have liked to tackle the cleaning and arranging immediately, but since our return had been late Friday evening, we had only Saturday to prepare for Sunday. We dared not hope for much of a turnout for Sunday services, but soldiers must always be ready.

Taking our places on the bamboo benches Sunday morning, we waited prayerfully for our little congregation to arrive. Again we were surprised as we watched the little *chapelle-école* fill to capacity, then to overflowing, both for the morning and evening service. Could we hope that this indicated a true hunger for the Word? We praised God for bringing us back.

The next week was full as Mary, with the help of Setefan, heated drum after drum of water for washing clothes. I got busy making a cupboard from poles and box boards so Mary could have a little more storage space. Then together we cleaned and whitewashed our main room, which then got its final touch with the bright curtains. Since it was Philip's birthday, Mary hurried to bake a cake. Soon we found ourselves seated at a candlelight dinner in a fresh, cheery little home. We could not have felt more joy and contentment had we been in a palace.

The following day Mary started teaching school, both for the Africans and Buddy, while I continued cleaning and whitewashing the *chapelle-école*, then with her help as soon as school was out. The next project to attack was our neglected garden.

When my birthday rolled around a week later, Mary was so exhausted she couldn't even attempt making a birthday cake. "We just can't do it this time," she told Setefan. But Setefan wouldn't hear of it. He got busy, and with Mary's instructions, he made most of it himself. I was touched by this thoughtfulness, and recognized that he was beginning to enjoy some of our customs.

Mary continued to keep busy by adding sewing to her list of projects. The mosquito nets were needing repairs, I needed BVD's, the children needed pajamas, and it was time to make shirts for the schoolboys. All the required yardage came out of the same old bolts of unbleached muslin.

I noticed that Mary was beginning to wear down. During school hours she'd give the boys exercises while she'd come in and lie down. Her hands were breaking out with severe eczema, and her face began to swell, causing her much pain. Her condition worsened until she was unable to get up. This meant I had to take over the school and the care of the children, which distressed her as much as the pain.

One morning she woke up to hear Buddy praying for his sick mother. After ending with "amen," he came to her bedside and commanded, "Mother, rise up on thy feet and walk." Surprisingly, she began to feel a little better that day. She would have liked to indulge in some reading, but her face was too swollen for her glasses. Little by little, while her skin peeled, the swelling went down and strength returned.

Buddy was now seven. His spiritual development was giving us much joy. One evening he prayed in a very grown-up, yet childish way, "I thank You that You have bought me from Satan, and now, I'm just in Your hands. You came to this old Satan's world to die for sinners." To us it sounded like a confession of faith, the answer to our prayers and the realization of a special promise Mary and I had claimed from God.

The next day we were disappointed when he had to be spanked. His mother suggested that he pray, "Grant that this spanking will do me good." Instead he prayed, "I grant you, that this spanking will do me good." Buddy needed few spankings after that. His faith and confidence in prayer caused us to wonder—and sometimes have some tense moments.

The family at home had sent a Montgomery Wards catalog that he enjoyed paging through, exclaiming at all the wonders it contained. At the time he had very few clothes, not just because he was growing fast, but because our system for washing clothes caused them to wear out quickly.

Looking one day at the children's clothes section of the catalog, he picked out a sailor suit that he pointed out to his mother as just what he would like. Mary looked at the price. It far exceeded our budget, so she closed the catalog and tried to distract him. But that evening, and every prayer time afterward, Buddy prayed that God would send that particular sailor suit. We wondered if we should forbid him to pray like that or encourage him to expect an answer.

Since Mary was better, I went back to trekking in the villages, while battling those painful separations and the fears. At one time, when Mary was feeling particularly fearful, I asked six watchmen to look out for her.

Once separated, we counted the days and hours till we would once again be together. Since Buddy was getting to be a good little walker, I'd take him along from time to time. Upon our return he'd display as much excitement at seeing his mother and baby brother as they did to see us. Soon Buddy was begging to go along with me all the time, but I made sure he stayed as often as possible with his mother, since he was company for her and a big help when she was sick.

While Mary battled her skin problems, along with other tropical diseases, I had some to face as well. My struggle was with recurring dysentery. As the illness became aggravated, we decided to go to Kikwit for a doctor's consultation. Thankfully, we now had the truck. The ride wasn't the most pleasant for someone with a fever, but it was easier than foot travel. A few days in Kikwit resulted in immense relief and afforded an opportunity to sail downriver to Leverville again. It also permitted us to relieve our coworkers at Kikwit by taking some of the services. The change benefited me and refreshed the whole family.

Though it was now only the fourteenth of May, friends at Kikwit were already making preparations for the conference to be held there in August. Again, we wondered if we'd make it.

The hurdles for the conference this year had changed. Mary wasn't feeling well. "I'm just not up to it this year," was a startling admission from my social Mary. I wondered what I could do for her.

On August 5, our porter brought the mail, which included two packages from America. When I brought the packages in Mary exclaimed, "This is my shot in the arm." It was like Christmas as we unpacked beautiful clothes and shoes for all. There were two cute outfits for Philip and, for Buddy, the much prayed for sailor suit! How we wished the family at home could have seen the effect of those packages.

That evening Mary wrote in her diary, "Guess we'll just have to go to Kikwit now, with all these pretty new clothes."

But on August 8, Buddy took sick with a bad cold and a high fever. On the ninth Mary wrote, "There is no thought of going to Kikwit now until Buddy gets stronger." Buddy struggled with this decision and showed impatience because he so wanted to go. The next day Mary wrote, "Buddy is a lot better, but still weak. He is quite reconciled to the idea that, if the Lord wants us to stay, we'll gladly stay." On the eleventh Mary wrote, "We put out the fleece today that, if Buddy's temperature is normal all day, we can go tomorrow. We washed and packed and have everything ready, but now I feel so bad myself that I wonder how I'll make it."

By 10:00 the next morning we were on our way to Kikwit. The highlight of the conference this year was our visits with the missionaries, and especially with the Ostraholms. There were also new missionaries there whom we hadn't yet met.

During the conference Mary wrote, "Had a little chat with Doctor today. It looks like we'll be going to Vanga in March." What she meant was: "In March we will be going to Vanga for the birth of our third child." We were excited and happy about this prospect and Mary was prepared to accept the discomforts in store for her, but we were becoming increasingly concerned about Buddy. He was still far from well.

By the time the conference was over, his feet were so swollen that he couldn't walk. We wondered what his trouble could be. We wished we'd asked Doctor Ostraholm's advice, but by now he'd already left. We decided to wait a few days. The next day his hands were swollen and by the following day he couldn't use his hands or walk and they were covered with ugly black spots. We decided to consult the doctor in Kikwit. He immediately diagnosed Buddy's illness as purpera, a rare disease in children that causes rheumatoid pain, swelling, and bleeding under the skin. The doctor didn't know what could have brought it on—an insect bite perhaps, or a bacterial infection. We had no previous knowledge of this illness, so we didn't know our Buddy would be lame and crippled for another year. Carrying him around, I called him my Mephibosheth. We were all learning that, sometimes, army boots are worn on crippled feet.

39

Ordinary Sandals
Extending Grace

Porters arrived...on his birthday...
carrying a very big package.
                                    Iwungu Nzamba
                                    1942

The family had adapted contentedly into life at Kangu.
So when the mail arrived one day with a temporary permit
to occupy two hectors (five acres) in Iwungu, there were
mixed feelings. How could we desert Kangu?

At the conference I'd proposed the possibility of someone's coming to Kangu—a proposition to which there was no
response. Kangu still had the stigma of being the worst post.
Some felt that we'd wasted our time in that deserted little
place.

We tried not to pay attention to such remarks. Both of us
felt that, even though it had been fearful and lonely, Kangu

had taught us many lessons. We'd learned to love and appreciate some of the customs of the Babunda tribe, and to sympathize with them in the difficult conditions of their lives—so full of suffering and fear.

Their little grass huts were meager protection from the harsh storms, accompanied with vicious thunder and lightning, which occurred frequently during the rainy season. We were surprised that more of the huts didn't blow over from the driving winds.

Existence was always just a step ahead of starvation. Women practiced what they termed the "ajax cycle." They prepared food that would barely last four days. For two days no food was served except to the men and to nursing babies. The only food the rest of the family ate was what they found by their own means: rats, flying ants, or other edibles in the forest. This was to teach the children survival. But the extended stomachs of those children proved that it was barely that.

To ease pain and suffering, the only recourse they had was the witch doctor. He took advantage of their misery and extremities by demanding exorbitant payment. These services, connected with sorcery and spiritism, carried worrisome side effects, plunging them into deeper pain and bondage.

It seemed like something strange or tragic was always happening. We frequently had the visit of an old man named Eyeng, whose house was on the edge of the village and thus nearest to us. He was a good-natured man and liked to talk.

One day he came wringing his hands, indicating great sorrow. "Come and see," he begged. He took me to his house and pointed to a tree that stood beside it. I looked up to see his son hanging from a branch. He had hung himself when the witch doctor cast a spell on him.

Another lesson I learned in Kangu is one I considered my wilderness lesson. Alone and isolated from other Christians and from uplifting messages from the Word of God, I feared that I was becoming spiritually depleted. I was, of course, preparing numerous messages, but these were of the most elementary evangelistic nature for those still needing a milk diet.

For this reason I sent off an order for books from Moody Press. We received, among other titles, a copy of *Romans Verse by Verse* by William R. Newell. Mary and I decided to read it together each evening when the children were in bed and while it was still daylight. We would set our native woven chairs outside on the sand and read our chapter. Once again the grace of God stood, but in a fresh way, as we discovered new facets to this mystery. We even devoured the notes that were more difficult to read in the twilight. We dared not bring out our kerosene lamp for fear of mosquitoes.

I was thrilled later when I learned that my father in California had, at the same time, made similar discoveries about God's grace while listening to the radio messages of Dr. M.R. Dehaan, founder of the Radio Bible Class. It would provide subject matter for much of our communication.

This new understanding of grace would affect my entire life and be the main focus of my ministry. "As every man hath received the gift, even so minister the same one to another, as good stewards of the manifold grace of God." This was Peter's advice in his first epistle, and it sounded good to me. (See First Peter 4:10 KJV.)

Another lesson learned from this experience was the power of the printed page. Had it not come all the way to little Kangu to quench the thirst of a dry heart?

While the official papers for our settling in Iwungu were being filled out, we were preparing for our second baptism and I was developing a nasty ulcer on my toe. It caused my whole foot to swell to such a point that I could no longer put on my shoe. So, from an old tire I cut out a pair of sandals that were loose-fitting and permitted me to walk. After the baptism, to get back from the river meant a three-mile hike uphill. We'd hardly begun climbing the hill when it began to pour. In no time we were soaked and the pain in my foot was intense. I'd planned to leave early the next day for Iwungu, but when I jumped out of bed I found that I was unable to walk. I waited rather impatiently a couple of days, and on the third set out for Iwungu, taking Buddy with me.

The week there was difficult as I measured and prepared for building, and tried to find workmen to help. At one point the pain was so severe I was tempted to go straight to the doctor in Kikwit, but knowing it would delay my return home to Mary and Philip, I decided against it.

Limping home that evening, Mary was particularly happy to see me because she was feeling so sick. She collapsed on her lame husband, hoping I'd be able to take over. Buddy's condition had also worsened, confining him to a deck chair. I hobbled around tending to Mary and the children as best I could. It was a month before I was able to put on a shoe.

As soon as Mary was up to it, I took her to see the spot I'd chosen to build our home. She expressed her pleasure in her diary with these words: "It surely is a lovely spot. By faith I see a home standing there overlooking the valley. In His time it will be." It provided the hope she needed to endure the next two difficult months.

Building the house meant leaving her alone for the entire week, while I stayed at Iwungu overseeing the construction and working long hours. With the help of some of the boys from Kangu, the work began to advance. The state officials also lent their weight by showing up from time to time and telling the men of Iwungu that if they didn't help us build and carry water, they'd have to go out collecting rubber.

With the coming and going between Kangu and Iwungu, Mary and I were able to send messages back and forth and she was able to send food regularly, which was a big help to me.

One evening when I was returning to the family in the late afternoon, Buddy got on his bike and rode out to meet me, then dropped the bike and ran to me. I was happy to see his enthusiasm, but saddened later when I saw his swollen feet. The exertion of riding the bike and running had caused the illness to flare up severely. I found it necessary to take his bike away. He wouldn't see it again for many months.

Again I realized that being separated from Mary and the family was becoming unbearable. I hated to take Mary away from our clean and cozy little house in Kangu to the rough old *sambola* in Iwungu Nzamba, but it was all I had to offer. After moving her and installing our stove on the veranda, she was happy and content.

That Sunday we held our first Sunday morning service at Iwungu Nzamba and were pleased to see a good number come from Kangu. We tried to encourage them to keep coming. We so wanted to see them stay fed and encouraged. Meanwhile Buddy's condition continued to be of concern. It saddened us to see our active son confined to a deck chair. Mary was at a loss as to what to give him to do to keep him quiet and content.

When his birthday came around she wanted it to be especially happy. She set about making him a cake, only to discover that she had no eggs. While she contemplated what she should do, a lad by the name of Ipuche came by and asked if she'd trade him a fishhook for some eggs. She immediately produced a fishhook and got on with making the cake.

The same day some porters arrived carrying a very big package from the mission station in Tchene. The missionaries had received a large quantity of children's books from an overstocked bookstore in America. Knowing that there was a sick boy at Iwungu, they immediately sent them on to us. Even had they known the exact date of his birthday, they couldn't have timed it better. Obedient to the Spirit, they had ministered grace to a young disciple in a far more abundant way than they could have imagined. The assortment included storybooks and activity books of all kinds—everything to keep a little boy confined to a deck chair happy and content for hours.

40

Tiny Shoes in God's Hands

Buddy put on a record and
went into an African dance.

Vanga
1942

When the time came to settle at Iwungu, Setefan and Rachel informed us that this time they would not be moving with us. The news came as a blow. Setefan had so faithfully followed us from Kafumba to Mangungu, and even—of all places—to Kangu. "Why, Setefan?" I wanted to know.

"We want to start working for the rubber company so we can eventually work our way up to a job in the city," replied Setefan. "This would please Rachel."

We looked at the couple sorrowfully. The U.T.M. was forwarding funds for the building project at Iwungu, but we ourselves had little to count on. Thus we had few benefits to offer other than our love and friendship. With heavy hearts we said good-bye to Setefan, Rachel, and little Santu. I think we must have felt a little like the apostle Paul when he wrote, "Demas, having loved this present world, has deserted me and gone to Thessalonica" (see 2 Tim. 4:10).

We later learned that Setefan was killed in an industrial accident while collecting rubber in the forest. Further reports stated that Rachel had fallen prey to materialism and grown cold to spiritual things, and that Santu had rebelled and run away from home.

Thankfully, help was provided for Mary now through Kalerki and Mbumbi, who offered to help cook and care for the children. At this time the load was heavy because Buddy, unable to walk, had to be carried. After the efficient help of Setefan, who could even bake bread, Mary had to go back to square one with the basics of sanitation. Mbumbi and Kalerki, though inexperienced, were willing to follow directions. This was a first step, and they could already relieve Mary of the strain of carrying the firewood needed for cooking and washing. So while I kept busy overseeing the building, the house crew "kept the home fires burning," which now included preparations for a new family member.

One of Mary's projects was a bassinet. We had in our possession a water-resistant trunk that included a removable basket. This proved convenient because we had only to remove the basket to have a bathtub. Though the basket served as storage, Mary now saw in it a dreamy pink and white bassinet. From her scraps of material she pulled out some white cotton flannel, strips of mosquito netting, and pink shoulder strap ribbon. By lining the basket with the white flannel and adding a ruffle of net with dainty pink bows, her dream came true.

Creating the rest of the layette was less satisfactory. With the same flannel material she made little nighties, but was disappointed with the result. They felt too stiff and harsh for a baby's skin. However, finding a blanket was even more difficult. Philip's baby blankets had been completely worn out and discarded. The only one left was a little ragged red blanket that was his *blankie*. Without it he couldn't sleep. What was she going to do?

Although she wondered about some of these practical aspects, she was troubled even more by something she confided only to her diary. "I hope we get to Vanga in time." Because I'd had difficulty in getting supplies and working with temperamental workmen, the building was going up slower than planned.

About that time a steady rain set in. I decided that the best use of time would be to stay home and sort out hinges and nails. I'd barely started when men came from Tshene with a note asking me to transport several women to Kikwit, where they were to make connections for going to Kafumba. This trip would involve going to Tshene to get them, bringing them home, putting them up for the night, then taking them to Kikwit. It meant that I'd be absent five days in all.

I noticed a look of anxiety in Mary's eyes. There was a moment of hesitation before she spoke. "I'll be okay. Take Buddy along," she encouraged me.

The following Sunday Mary didn't feel up to leading the service so she let the boys from Kangu take over. Though they needed some prompting and preparation, in the end they did remarkably well. It was just a tiny evidence that the Church was going forward.

That afternoon a violent storm broke out. Rain beat down as thunder roared and lightning crisscrossed the skies. Kalerki and Mbumbi came to her trembling with fear. Taking Philip onto her lap, the four huddled together.

Mary glanced out the window, just as lightning struck a palm tree. Sparks flew out of the top branches as the lightning ran down the trunk and into the ground. It proved to be an excellent conductor.

They were much relieved, late in the evening the next day, to see the truck driving up. I was pleased to have with me a birthday gift for Mary that I knew would please her. It was an eggbeater given to me by the Streets, as they had received two.

Mary was overjoyed when I presented the little tool to her. It would prove to be, apart from her cookstove, her main labor-saving appliance. From then on the trusted eggbeater went everywhere with us. Even in later years, when given an electric beater, she'd smile sheepishly at the family and, instead of using the sophisticated beater, reach for the trusted old eggbeater. "I'm not used to power tools," she'd say apologetically as she vigorously turned the well-worn handle.

I stepped up work on building the house as Mary was anxious to get moved before the arrival of the baby. On February 9, though the new house wasn't yet completed, I told Mary she could start packing. We could take over a couple of loads. Once we began moving, though, we just kept going. Before night fell we were completely moved. There were many battles before us, but we felt like we'd entered the promised land.

The next day we had an unplanned housewarming party when our friends the Eichers, and then a group from Mukedi, drove in on their way to Kikwit. Mary hurried to get dinner and we had a joyful time together.

The following day, both Mary and Buddy looked peaked. I was getting alarmed. Time was running out. I hurried to lay down a bamboo mat in another room that would serve as our dining room, while Mary tried to get organized enough to bake a cake for Philip's second birthday. This was a little harder than she'd expected as people were working around her, finishing doors and whitewashing walls.

We also were trying to get a third room completed so we could provide comfortable lodging for Miss Johanson, a nurse from Kinchua. She was to come and stay with us, then go with us to Vanga, since the Vanga hospital was short-staffed and we needed someone to look after Phil.

A few days later, as I was waking up, Mary wished me "Happy Birthday." A few minutes later, however, when we looked at the calendar, we noticed that it was not February 19 as we had thought, but February 20. We'd been so busy that we'd completely lost a day.

"You've got enough to do today," I told her. "Don't try to bake a cake. Use the time rather to rest."

"No, better late than never," she insisted as she got up and went to the kitchen. In no time the new eggbeater was out and she was busy stirring up my cake. It was the only way she had to make the day special.

I was relieved that I didn't have to go and get Miss Johanson from the Kinchua mission station. Our friend Mr. Vermeilen, who was a company worker, offered to do this for me. Mary and I were relieved when they drove in. Miss Johanson's room was all prepared and ready for her.

The first days of March while I made shutters for the windows, Mary started sorting and packing for the trip to Vanga. We would not only need clothes, but also food and supplies for the journey and for the stay in Vanga.

She'd barely begun when she doubled over with pain. Panic showed in her face. Even though we had a nurse in the house, she longed for the reassuring presence of our beloved physician, Dr. Ostraholm. The next few days she continued packing, between intervals of rest, while I tried to reassure her. The close call she'd had after the birth of our Buddy had made her apprehensive. Fears are sometimes learned. How different we both were from the reckless young couple we'd been when awaiting our first child.

Though unwilling to admit it to Mary, I was struggling with a giant fear myself. If something should go wrong, who would be to blame? Neither of us spoke to each other about these fears. Kneeling together, we committed ourselves to God. All is well in the Father's hands.

With a sense of relief we left Iwungu on the fourth, but there was still a long truck ride to Vanga. After a few days in Kikwit, we continued to Vanga, arriving there late on the evening of the eleventh.

Once there, Mary began to relax, and baby decided there was no rush after all. She wrote in her diary, "I'm so surprised that I don't feel worse after that long truck drive...I'm so much better since arriving here...Everyone is so kind and friendly and it's pleasant." We unpacked leisurely and enjoyed the company of our Vanga friends. The Smiths, who'd been at Vanga for the birth of their first child, which coincided with the birth of our Philip, were there again awaiting another birth. Doctor called us "his repeaters."

Mary had time for some reading and I was able to fix Doctor's car before baby showed any sign of wanting to come. Meanwhile Mrs. Ostraholm checked out the layette Mary had brought. Shaking her head, she went off for a search in her attic. A while later she returned, her arms full of blankets and tiny clothes. Both women were excited and happy. Mrs. Ostraholm had been waiting for someone who'd appreciate the things she'd put away and Mary was thrilled to have a complete layette. We were finally ready for baby.

On the twenty-second, we called the doctor thinking that something was going to happen soon, but it wasn't till 5:00 the next morning that our baby girl put in her appearance. We named her Joanne Elizabeth after Mary's brother John and her two sisters, Anna and Elizabeth.

Buddy was overjoyed when he heard he had a baby sister. He dashed over to the hand-crank phonograph player someone had left in the guest house, put on a lively record, and went into an African dance. "Baby sister you've come at last, I prayed for you and now I have you," he sang in a frenzy of excitement.

Mary had her own special prayer of thanksgiving as she examined the baby's tiny feet. "Praise God she doesn't have her mother's feet," she whispered. As ridiculous a prayer as it may have seemed, she'd been praying that her daughter would have dainty feet instead of long boats like her mother. To that prayer, I'm sure God smiled and answered "yes."

"There's been so much rejoicing over our daughter," Mary wrote in her diary.

41

Everyday Shoes
on Sacred Ground

Birds delighted us with song...
singing "Bless them...keep them."
Iwungu Nzamba
1942

Buddy's excitement over the arrival of baby Joanne was tamed when his illness flared up the same day. Blackish spots appeared on his body, while his face became swollen and took on a bluish look. We were glad to be near the doctor so he could see how the illness acted. Doctor decided the problem was due primarily to a lack of iron and began treatment immediately.

Though anxious to get back to Iwungu and settle into our new home with our new family member, we felt that we needed to take advantage of the medical help available to us at Vanga. So we stayed longer than planned.

Mary and Buddy convalesced on deck chairs, while I tried to cope with household chores and Philip, who'd become hard to manage. We had hoped that Miss Johanson, the nurse we had brought from Kinchua, could care for him, but he didn't take to her at all.

She wanted him to look nice all the time, and to go for walks with her. He didn't appreciate all her attentions to dress him just so, and to keep his hair combed and face and hands clean. He would immediately run his hands through his hair and run out to play in the dirt. We were at a loss at what to do, especially since we didn't want to offend Miss Johanson. We need not have worried because Miss Johanson suddenly took ill with a fever and was obliged to stay in bed. By that time Mary was able to give Philip the attention only she could give.

Soon after returning to Iwungu, we inherited a dog which the children named Micky. Philip was captivated by the little animal, and it was evident that his affection was amply returned. Then, when Micky had five pups, he was even more thrilled. We would soon discover that all animals seemed to gravitate toward him. Meanwhile, we could tell that his life was full and happy with a new sister, new playmates, and six new dogs.

For Mary and me, it was time to get organized and to move forward with the work. Since we hadn't properly unpacked before leaving for Vanga, there was a lot of work for Mary to do in the house, besides caring for the children and teaching Buddy, now that he was getting stronger. For me there was still a lot of building to do, starting with the chapel and then houses for the boys who'd come from Kangu. The Mennonite Brethren had sent a generous contribution for this project, which I wanted to see completed so we could get on with regular services and teaching.

While awaiting the completion of the chapel, we discovered a spot that became almost sacred in our eyes. Near our house was a group of shady trees that resembled an orchard, or grove, since they weren't fruit trees. After we'd taken out the tall grass and planted a lawn, it took on the appearance of a park. It was a cool and refreshing place to eat our evening meal and to hold services, and was a safe place for our children to play. I built a little fence around it, and it served as a large playpen for the baby.

Birds flew around in the branches above and delighted us with song. Sometimes Philip would stop suddenly in the middle of his play, look up, listen, then exclaim, "They're singing 'bless them...keep them.' " Mary and I smiled in agreement. Truly it did sound just like that.

As clouds began to gather over our heads, the reality of those words comforted and quieted our restless, troubled hearts. Though darkness was settling around us, we could follow the example of our little son and lift up our faces to the Giver of every blessing.

42

Disability Shoes Bouncing on a Sea of Love

Mary and I looked up, and seeing only
darkness, had but one question: "Why?"
Iwungu Nzamba to Ilebo and back
1942

We'd hardly settled into Iwungu, when storm clouds
gathered above us. What could they mean? Had we known
that those clouds were full of mercy drops, we could have
saved ourselves a lot of fretting and stewing. Sometimes
God's care and intricate plans of deliverance are veiled in
sweeping fog and stormy gales. Mary and I looked up, and seeing only darkness, had but one question on our lips: "Why?"

Now that we were ready to move forward, Mary was sick
again. Her feet became very swollen, then cracked open,

forming deep crevices that oozed with infection. In the tropics, infection spreads rapidly. In a short time, it had spread up to her knees. Her legs and feet had to be wrapped in bandages, and before long she was confined to her bed. A trip to the doctor in Kikwit hadn't brought the hoped-for relief. In fact, the prescribed medication only seemed to aggravate her problem.

I now faced another difficult decision. With workmen waiting for me at Iwungu, I was needed there; yet it was apparent that Mary needed to be under a doctor's care for a longer period of time. How could I care for the small children without her, and how would they get along without their mother? The decision I made, I knew, would be inconvenient for each family member. Mary would stay at Kikwit with the two little ones, and I would bring Buddy back with me to Iwungu.

I took the family to Kikwit where the doctor prescribed a treatment of injections, and assured me that he himself would come daily to the mission house to administer them. With tear-filled eyes our family split. "I'll be back in a week," I assured them. "We can start counting the days."

Upon my return I consulted privately with the doctor. "What prognosis can you give?" I asked.

"Only the Great Physician can heal her," he replied. "Frankly, I don't think she'll ever walk again."

I looked at the doctor with unbelieving eyes. "We'll continue the treatment for a few more weeks," he said. "That's all I can do for her." I sat in the truck by myself for a while, trying to grasp the hard facts and seeking counsel from that "Great Physician."

When I joined Mary, she wanted to know what the doctor had said. I decided to tell her the truth. Then I suggested taking Philip back with me. "Maybe if you get more rest, you'll start to heal. Kalerki and Mbumbi are trustworthy. They'll help me care for Philip. He'll be all right."

"I guess it's the only way," Mary reluctantly agreed.

Our separation was even harder this time. From her window Mary waved and watched as we climbed the hill and crossed the river. Philip, walking beside me, seemed such a little boy to be separated from his mother.

After three weeks, Mary was showing marked improvement. We were happily preparing to return, all together this time, when things got lively around us. A missionary dentist, Dr. Smith, had just driven up with Mr. Miller, whose daughter Marian had broken her arm.

With all the excitement over this, it was late when we finally got off, accompanied by Mr. Miller, Marian, Mr. Jantz, and Dr. Smith. We didn't make it to the river before dark and before a storm. That particular ferry had a motor powerful enough to withstand the strong current, but just as we reached the middle of the river, the motor gave out. We drifted downstream, carried by the current and the storm. The experience was frightening, but didn't shake us so much as the hidden storm that was about to burst.

The following afternoon, as we were conversing, Mr. Miller proposed that, because of our health problems, we should go to a place with a more favorable climate—or home on furlough—and let them take over Iwungu. Nothing could have struck with stronger impact. Mary and I were suddenly plunged into a dark and foreboding storm.

We'd just entered our "promised land." Was all the waiting, all the time in Kangu, in vain? With all the living in *sambolas*, we'd just moved into a house with a minimum of comfort and suited for our family. That evening, after our return to Iwungu, Mary wrote in her diary, "Abe has fixed the house so nice, and it's such a joy to be here. I feel like I want to stay awhile and not think of going away. It gives me unrest and sorrow to think of going anywhere."

As Mary's condition improved, we thought the dark clouds would blow away. She was up and about and even taking on extra tasks, such as canning goat meat and making jam. The chapel was being completed and the children were happy. Mary was especially happy when little Philip went around singing, "Pray the clouds away" and "Joy, joy, joy down in my heart."

The Jantz family had invited us for Thanksgiving, which Mary was looking forward to now that she was feeling so much better. We had a lovely dinner and fellowship with them. When we went to see the doctor, he was shocked to see Mary walk in. "*Madame, Madame,*" he exclaimed. "*C'est un miracle!*" She was wearing a pair of sandals that Mr. Peterson, another missionary, had taken off his own feet and given to her. They were most appreciated as they were the only shoes around that fit her grotesquely swollen feet.

The doctor, though pleased with her improvement, was serious. "Have you considered a change of climate?" he asked.

There it was again. Just when we thought the storm was behind us.

A few days later the Miller family came. This time we braced ourselves for the worst.

Mary had been sure that her improvement was a sign that we would be staying. She was deeply troubled. I was beginning to have mixed feelings. I didn't want to take the doctor's words lightly. Then too, the Miller family had a large church backing them, allowing them considerable financial freedom. Perhaps they were more in a position to develop Iwungu than we were.

It was still wartime. Many missionaries were having a hard time surviving because of tightened finances in America. Our friends the Whitakers, as well as us, were among those who were practically without resources. The Whitakers had gone to the copper mining town of Chingola near Elizabethville on the Rhodesian border. Charles Whitaker had taken employment in the mines to support his family while continuing a Bible teaching ministry on the side.

A month later, at the Kamayala conference, we stayed in the house the Whitakers had occupied. It brought back many memories to be there, celebrating Buddy's birthday in the very house where he had been born. A cake was made for him, and we were thankful that he was now in good health and able to enjoy all the celebrations and activities going on.

The highlight of this conference was a touching and unforgettable message by Mr. Grinks, a missionary whom I'd never had the privilege of meeting, but who had stirred my curiosity.

While Mary and I were at Kafumba, a porter had brought a letter from him addressed to all the missionaries there. The first words of the letter were still fresh in my mind, "We're on our way to heaven via Kikanji." The words weren't trite, for the family had just been rescued along the African coast by a Dutch freighter after the Portuguese ship they were sailing on was sunk.

I'd heard much about this unusual missionary, whose wife had since died of blackwater fever, leaving him with five children. His message, which included his testimony, was entitled "Three Graves": one—burial with Christ in baptism; two—burial at sea of his family's elaborate outfit of a car, a trailer, and expensive woodworking tools; and three—burial of his wife in an African grave.

As I pondered the experiences of this brother, the burial of my dreams for Iwungu seemed small.

Mary had once again become ill and was unable to attend any of the meetings. Several large boils had developed on her neck, and she was unable to stay on her feet. Others suggested we take a furlough or join the Whitakers for a time in the cooler Rhodesian climate. Before, their suggestions had seemed cruel. Now I was beginning to wonder if a Divine hand was on the handle of a door. I gently shared my feelings with Mary.

By now I'd fixed up the second truck that I'd originally bought for parts. It had been a long slow process because I had to wait for parts to arrive from Sam Reimer, my brother-in-law in Oregon. Mr. Vermeylen, our Portuguese friend, who often visited us with his family, had repeatedly shown interest in these trucks. He had even asked to buy them. I kept putting him off, till one day Mary and I decided we'd ask an exorbitant price of 50,000 francs, or $1,000. If he accepted, we'd sell. To our amazement he accepted our offer and the money was safely put in the bank. We didn't know, at that precise moment, that we were depositing our boat ticket to America.

We decided to pay a visit to the Whitakers. Boarding the boat in Kikwit, we were comforted with the memory of the previous Sunday when a man named Mann had made an open confession of faith. We were also grateful that Makwalenge had agreed to accompany us to Léopoldville, to help with the cooking and washing along the way.

When the boat stopped at Lunungu beach, we got off and walked to Vanga, surprising the folks there. After enjoying a lovely evening of fellowship and catching up on the changes in the children, the friends got together supplies of all kinds and presented them to us. Mary was especially happy for the groceries, and their thoughtfulness lifted our sagging spirits.

In Léopoldville, we renewed our passports and enjoyed fellowship with the Baiottis, rejoicing with them that Mr. Baiotti had been released from prison. When we boarded a boat for Port Franqui, we sadly said "good-bye" to Makwalenge. He had been such a help to us along the way, and we'd miss him very much on the next stage of our journey.

The ride on the riverboat was difficult with the children. The heat during the day with the sun and the boilers was almost unbearable, and the contrasting cool night air was dangerous. Philip soon developed a cough, then became very ill. When we reached a town called Bosongo, we all got off to see if we could find a doctor. The one we found was good to the children; he gave medicine to Philip. Our son began to recover, but by the time we were completing the boat trip, baby Joanne was developing a bad cough.

In Ilebo[1] there was a nice clean hotel where we went to celebrate Philip's birthday, then boarded the train for Elizabethville by 8:00 that evening.

When we reached Elizabethville three days later, we could hardly wait to get our baby to the hospital. She now had a high fever and her breath was coming fast and quick. The doctor immediately gave injections of quinine and camphor. But seeing how ill she was, he resorted, for the first time in his life, to antibiotics; to these she responded immediately, much to everyone's relief. Mary stayed with her in the hospital for eight days while the boys and I slept in a dismal, dirty hotel.

As I was walking the streets of Elizabethville with the boys, I came across an old Packard that was for sale. It had a good body, but I was a little too optimistic about the engine. Having just made a good deal on the sale of the trucks, I figured there was no harm in buying it; if it needed a little fixing, I could do that and then sell it easily.

This time, however, I miscalculated. The car proved to be a lemon and gave us many problems. Still, it made at least this last part of the trip to Chingola more comfortable for the family.

We had good times of fellowship with the Whitakers and other missionaries there, who took us around and showed us generous hospitality. We especially enjoyed the English-speaking Sunday school and church where I was asked to preach several times. However, after visiting the mines and considering secular work, I knew it was not what God wanted us to do. I felt more strongly than ever my calling to proclaim the gospel, and had renewed assurance that God would surely supply the needs of my family.

At the same time, we considered the possibility of returning on furlough, but found that all the boats were booked up

---

1.   Port Franqui

and we'd have to wait for several months. We decided to return to Iwungu and wait for the next orders from Supreme Headquarters. Mary wrote in her diary: "Our stops, as well as our goes, are ordered of the Lord."

Our trip back to Iwungu was quite eventful. the car did all right for the first 100 miles; I babied it along for another 80, after which she decided to quit—miles from nowhere. It was now 11:00 p.m. and the nearest settlement of any kind was a monastery of Dominican monks where we sent for help.

A priest from Mababi Kasari finally arrived by 2:30 the next afternoon, and he kindly towed us to Lubudi while they put up the family in the monastery. The children were exhausted after spending the night in the bush. Mary wrote in her diary that evening, "It's Joanne's birthday, and in what a place we are!"

From there we prayed the car to Idiofa, where we later sold it. Since we were near the Kinchua mission station, which we had never visited, we decided to take a little side trip to see the missionaries there.

When we arrived at Kinchua—by way of porters—we found the atmosphere tense from some unresolved problems and misunderstandings among the missionaries. It exploded when one of the missionaries asked me to take a look at her clock, which wasn't working right. Somehow my looking at the clock opened a vent for compressed steam that had been building up for some time. Hopefully, airing the problem helped to identify and resolve some of the issues, but I wouldn't hesitate to affirm that all of us missionaries are not necessarily angels, even though both are messengers.

After a time of prayer, discussion, and the innocent and winning ways of our children, the atmosphere improved.

We were glad to get back to Iwungu three weeks later, but sad when we saw how run-down things had become. We immediately got busy cleaning and tidying and before we knew it, we were going full speed ahead.

I translated a memory plan of all the major doctrines and began Bible studies, including a memory plan, while Mary went back to teaching school. A day that would particularly stand out in our memories was when we went to the river for our first baptism at Iwungu. Five men were baptized, including Ympwaka, a blind man.

During these days, however, our hearts were often perplexed about our future. The children were now frequently sick, especially baby Joanne who remained fragile after having pneumonia in Elizabethville. We'd now sold our car and kept our belongings half-packed, since the Millers were anxious to move in. Seeing so many evidences of God's blessing on our efforts, though, we decided to stay at least until the following April.

However, on July 31, as I was putting the roof on another house, we received a telegram from the family in Oregon. Our home church had advanced funds toward return tickets. They wanted us to come home.

We were getting a cable ready to send back to tell them we'd decided to wait till April when another wire arrived telling of further arrangements. We decided to accept these plans as the official and final word from Headquarters.

The following week was exceptionally busy as I wanted very much to complete the last buildings and Mary wanted to leave presents with the schoolchildren who had worked so hard. The garden was full of vegetables, the house was clean with a fresh coating of whitewash, and Mary was all organized for another week of school. But as Mary wrote that evening: "He leads and we follow."

The last Sunday was particularly blessed as the Lord gave us peace. Later we'd realize that our vision and claim to the promise, "The land I will give you," was far too limited in God's eyes. He has ways of adding overflowing abundance to our pitiful little requests, but en route to the promised land we must weather storms that block out the vision and thrust us into predicaments where we have no alternative but to trust Him. As far as Iwungu Nzamba was concerned, God had prepared others to harvest where we'd sown in weakness and tears. Someday we'll rejoice together. The Millers were destined to replace us—until matters of health would prompt them to move on—to be replaced by the Smiths and the Yosts, all of whom were dedicated and gifted servants of God.

When the truck came to take us away, we didn't look back. We knew God's plans for us were for our good, and the wisdom of His design was soon to be unveiled to us.

43

Traveling Shoes
With Journey Mercies

Relieved and delighted, we hopped aboard.
Iwungu Nzamba to Sazaire to Portugal
August 9—November 24, 1943

On the ninth of August, 1943, we hitched a ride on a Cordoza company truck on its way to Kikwit. About halfway there we met Mr. Janzen who, knowing we didn't have transportation, was coming to get us and offered to store our things at Kafumba. Relieved and delighted, we hopped aboard.

We went to Kikwit first to take care of some business and to share the main concern of the station: Mrs. Jantz was now seriously ill. How well we understood. Then we took an extra jog to Kafumba where we would store some belongings. Much had changed since our beginnings there in 1933. Two graves had been added to the cemetery. The first was Mrs.

Ernestina Janzen, who had served Africa 21 years. We remembered how she'd coached us in our first steps. Now, six years after her death, Aaron had just married Martha Hiebert. The second grave was that of Martha Manz, who'd died two years ago of malaria. With only two years of service, her highest contribution to Africa had been her death. Giving life itself is the greatest proof of love. In spite of these casualties, the work was moving right ahead.

Mary enjoyed some long talks with Martha Janzen as they walked around the mission station, seeing the houses, talking with old friends, and being introduced to new. As they passed the palm oil factory, Mary become violently ill. "It's strange," she apologized, "the smell of palm oil never bothered me before."

"I wonder, Mary," responded Martha Janzen sympathetically, "if you aren't expecting baby number four."

Her speculation was accurate. We now knew why we must reach America before April, as previously planned, and the sooner the better. With Mary's frail condition, having another baby in Africa could prove disastrous.

When we returned to Kikwit, where we were to catch the boat, we found the mission house full to capacity—and no boat was scheduled to leave for another week. We squeezed in and tried to be patient. Meanwhile Joanne had a swelling behind her ear and a soaring fever. The treatment the doctor prescribed didn't seem to help, so the day before we were to leave, the doctor lanced her ear and advised us not to go.

Since Mary was sharing a room with other women, there was lots of noise and activity around them. They didn't seem to be getting much rest, so I thought it best to go on to Leverville where there was a good hospital.

In saying good-bye to the Jantz's, we found, to our relief, that Mrs. Jantz was much improved. Again we prayed that God would heal her. So many people out there were waiting for her ministering hands, and she loved to minister.

Mr. Eicher took us to the port at 5:15 the next morning where, accompanied by Kalerki and Mbumbi, we boarded the steamboat. When we arrived at Leverville three hours later, we went directly to the hospital. The sisters there were most kind. After dressing Joanne's ear, they took us home for dinner.

By five that evening we were once more on the boat headed for Léopoldville. We arrived at Vanga that evening before dark where our beloved physician, Dr. Ostraholm, checked Joanne's ear and told us how to care for her. Once more the Vanga friends saw us to the boat, which would be home for us for five more days.

In Léopoldville we found housing at the Salvation Army headquarters. We'd hoped that our stay there would be brief, but it stretched over a month and a half while we waited for a Portuguese visa. Because of the war, it was safer to go through neutral Portugal than by way of Belgium or France.

I was happy that Mary was getting the much needed rest; we also found a doctor who assured us that Joanne was getting better. This became evident as we watched our little ones play. Philip, concerned about his limp baby sister, would tease her by making faces at her, or darting in and out of her view. When his shenanigans got the response "peek-a-boo Philipoo," we knew she was on the mend.

We all enjoyed moments of fellowship with the Becquets, the couple in charge of the Salvation Army headquarters. Our Philip delighted Mr. Becquet, the commanding officer, by responding to the typical "hallelujah" greeting with a loud soldier-like "hallelujah" of his own. Mr. Becquet was also interested in our boys Kalerki and Mbumbi who, being straight from the bush, were quite different from the people in the city. To our delight he made sure they had a comfortable place to stay and that they were well fed. This was to be the place where we would part company with these two dear boys. It was comforting to know that, in a sense, they were taking part of us back to Iwungu Nzamba and Kangu, while we were taking them with us in our hearts and prayers.

We were able to spend some time with our Italian friends the Baiottis and to get to know another couple, the Mathyssens. All these people seemed to be showering us with kindness—to which Mary didn't know quite how to respond. Being straight from the bush, our clothes were worn from the harsh washing and were far from normal standards of civilization. Also, with her bandages, it was evident that her health was below par. But as the wives had opportunities to chat and discuss matters of spiritual depth, she began to relax and let down her defenses. When Mary showed interest in their knitting, they offered to teach her. Mary enthusiastically accepted. Before long they could be heard laughing and joking in typical sisterly fashion.

Now Mary could receive their kindnesses as tokens of love rather than of pity. There were dinner invitations, outings in the city, and once a cake was sent over by Mrs. Baiotti when we knew she wasn't feeling well. Then a little sweater was presented to Mary for Joanne. Unknown to us, the knitting needles had been clicking on our behalf. Another day we responded to a knock on the door and found a woman standing with her arms full of gifts. She introduced herself as Madame Manot, and explained that she'd come from the opposite side of Léopoldville in the part called Kinshasha. Seeing how happy these people were in doing things for us, we began to realize that our needs were becoming opportunities for blessing them.

I was kept busy speaking at meetings conducted by the Salvation Army and other groups, and tending to business matters, which included frequent trips to the Portuguese consulate.

Finally, on October 15, we received our steamship ticket, our passport with the visa, and our train ticket to Lufu Gare. There was great rejoicing on the part of the friends there when we finally had all these papers in hand, but when we said "good-bye," there were mixed feelings.

After an early breakfast in the home of the Mathyssens, the Becquets took us to the station, helped us put our luggage on the train, and made sure we were comfortable. Then we bowed our heads as Mr. Becquet asked the Lord's blessing on the next lap of our journey.

We continued to Mbange Manteke where we had received an invitation from Mr. and Mrs. Engwall, the missionaries there. Here a whole house was made available to us for our use. Our hosts took us around to see the work being done and some points of interest. It was all so different compared to the villages and houses from which we'd come.

We were taken out to the old hill site, which was the original station of Mbanga Manteke. It also was the first mission station established in the Congo. Being there over the weekend, I was asked to speak in their morning service and also at the leper camp, which was a rich experience and privilege.

After a wonderful time of refreshment with more new friends, Mr. Engwall drove us to the Swedish mission station of Lufu Gare. Here we were able to write and mail out many letters, and prepare ourselves for boarding the motor launch that would take us to the steamship in Sazaire.

The ride to the steamship was supposed to take only a few hours, but the launch was having motor trouble. As the hours slipped by we were forced to spend the night on hard benches, using life belts for cushions. Philip especially couldn't settle down and, crying most of the night, he kept everyone awake.

When we finally reached Sazaire we were informed that the boat would not be coming that day. The children were hungry, tired, and irritable when we took them to a dumpy hotel with a bumpy bed. Early the next morning, after a hurried breakfast, they rushed us off to the beach—to wait till 11:00—for the delayed boat.

It was almost noon when a motor launch finally pulled up. The children were piled in and we headed out to deep water where our steamship, the *Colonial* was waiting to take us aboard. Boarding the steamship was a little more difficult than walking across a gangplank. Sitting in our little boat as it bounced on the waves, I wondered how the family would reach the deck of that giant steamship. As we all watched with wonder, a rope ladder was let down to our motor launch and we were told to watch for the change between the swelling and ebbing of the waves. At that moment we were to grab tightly to the rope, wait for a dip in the wave, and jump. Once separated from the motor launch, we had to climb the ladder, while hanging over the open sea with waves below beating against the ship. An officer carried up Philip and Joanne, but the rest of us had our first experience as marine acrobats. For my brave *Mama Mbote*, now large with child, it was a daunting challenge.

The cabin, designed for three passengers, seemed no bigger than a shoe box. The deck was small for active children too, but at least we were moving.

We became acquainted with some other passengers, Mr. and Mrs. Oline, who were Swedish missionaries. Older and wiser than we, they seemed to take over where the Becquets left off. Mrs. Oline got out her knitting needles and quickly made sweaters for our thinly clad children.

The food took some adjusting to, particularly on the part of the children. They weren't accustomed to the seasonings, especially the flavor of olive oil, which was poured over everything. They picked and played with their food and when told that the special dish before them was stomach, they turned up their noses. Had it been smelly *makayabe* or lucu with *sucka-sucka* greens, they would have dived in. We learned that meat was not stocked in refrigerators, but by livestock on the hoof.

The voyage was smooth as we left the tropics, passing Dakar, then the sixteenth degree line, and on to Madeira.

Here the ship unloaded cargo. While there we saw a convoy of 23 warships, a grim reminder that a war was going on. Forty-eight hours later the ship docked at Lisbon. God's traveling mercies had followed us all the way to Portugal. We were thankful to walk across a plank to dry land. Gusts of icy winds now jolted us to the fact that we were in Europe and that it was winter.

44

Following Shoes Behind the Man With the Pitcher

How does one find lodging for
a family of five in a strange country?

Lisbon, Portugal
1943

My primary concern as we stepped off the ship was lodging. How does one find lodging for a family of five (and a half) in a foreign country, where a foreign language is spoken, where you have little money in the currency of the country, and where you have no friends?

From my Bible reading I'd been particularly impressed with the story of Jesus' last Passover celebration with His disciples. In giving directions for the needed preparations, Jesus instructed, "Follow the man with the pitcher." (See Mark

14:13.) I liked the sound of that phrase. For me, it seemed like a good principle to apply when human wisdom is inadequate and when one is looking for a clue, a signpost, or a providential finger. In times like those I'd pray, "Please show me the man with the pitcher." This was a moment when that prayer seemed opportune.

Friends in Elizabethville had given me a few addresses, but I didn't know if they were still current or how I'd be received. I picked up the first and, leaving Buddy in charge of the baggage, I went searching for the address.

It happened to be that of an American missionary. When I introduced myself, he excused himself for being ill, but offered to take me and my family to the home of Mr. and Mrs. Mathey, a Swiss couple who operated a bookstore in Lisbon.

Immediately I ran back to the family and announced, "Come, I've found the man with the pitcher."

We collected our baggage and followed "our man" to the home of the Matheys. There we were given a much appreciated cup of hot tea. After visiting with us for a while, they took us to a boarding house on Rua San Paulo.

Our first concern was finding warm clothes for the children. The room we were given at the boarding house had only a little kerosene heater that we couldn't afford to keep refilling. The freezing temperatures were unusual for Portugal and for that time of the year. To us it felt as though we'd stepped into a deep freeze. Philip could now wear the snowsuit Buddy had worn on our first furlough, so he was warm, but Buddy and Joanne had no coats. We were able to find a jacket we could afford for Buddy, but that left little money over for Joanne. We'd just have to bundle her up as best we could. Buddy, having only cotton shorts, also needed trousers. Again the price was out of reach.

The next day I went out alone and found some material. A missionary staying at the boarding house offered Mary the use of her sewing machine, so Mary, with her trouser-making experience, was able to produce the trousers in record time.

We were hoping our stay in Portugal would be brief. Surely it wouldn't take more than just a few days to board another ship bound for Philadelphia, but again a lesson in patience was due. God's schedule for the Kroeker family included a four-week stay in Portugal.

Unknown to us, the Portuguese shipping company had planned to have us wait in Lisbon for one of their ships coming from Korea, but with the war, the ship never came. The company finally agreed to transfer our passage money to another company, but when I returned to make sure everything was in order, it appeared that nothing had been done at all. Meanwhile we'd run out of *escondidos*—and it was impossible to get money exchanged.

I went to the American embassy in the hopes they could help us, but it proved to no avail. So I went to the British embassy. They too apologized with, "We can't exchange your money, but we could lend you some that you can pay back to us when you reach America."

We didn't know what to do—so we prayed. The Lord answered by touching the heart of a Mr. Brown, who was working with the British ligation. Seeing our predicament—no doubt we looked pitiful enough—he offered to assist us. By putting pressure on the Colonial Line, he managed to get them to refund our passage to Philadelphia, with the exception of 3200 esc. which they claimed for commission.

After transferring 33,000 esc. to a second company, the National Line, we soon discovered that they had a similar problem and couldn't give us a definite reservation.

Finally Mr. Brown suggested transferring to a third company. At this point the second company claimed *their* generous commission, which would make our funds inadequate. By now Mr. Brown was sufficiently upset to pull out all stops in his negotiating and would not settle until he was successful in getting all our money transferred with no commission to any company and had our tickets in his hands.

Meanwhile we'd made the acquaintance of several people at the Brethren church who invited us to their homes for meals, especially the Mattheys. They brought us several times to their house to warm up by their coal stove. Buddy enjoyed playing with their son Pierre, who was about his age.

The Mattheys proudly told us about the experiences their Pierre had been having at school. His young friends had discovered that he knew a lot about God and the Bible. When questions were asked, Pierre would reply with the simple, direct answers he'd been given by his parents. Coming home from school one day, Pierre was concerned. "Mother," he said, "we must pray that God will send them a missionary."

To this his mother replied, "Pierre, you are that missionary."

We thrilled with them over this newly appointed missionary to Lisbon's Elementary School. There are no age requirements in God's application forms for missionary service. He accepts all—from the very young to the very old.

The Mattheys also invited us to their church's Christmas program scheduled for the nineteenth. Here, to our wonder and shock, the women presented Joanne with a beautiful warm wool coat the ladies had made themselves, along with warm pants and a little hat. Mary lost no time in dressing Joanne. To the delight of all it fit perfectly; the soft blue suited her fair skin and hair. When she showed her pleasure by stroking her sides and looking up with a big smile, the ladies cried.

We were anxious, at this time, to hear how Belgium was getting along in the war. We'd received no news from any of our friends there for a long time. The Mattheys explained to us the project the Christians in Portugal had taken on, which was to send sardines to Belgium where food supplies were rationed or cut off. When our money came through, we were happy to be able to participate in this project while we intensified our prayers for our Belgian friends.

By this time it was evident that our departure time had come. On the morning of the twenty-second the Mattheys came to say good-bye. The moment of prayer was so moving and so sacred that Mary called it "a sweet benediction." Portugal would never again be "just a place on the map."

We went on board the SS *Saint Thomé* at 4:00 p.m. and were on our way soon after. Our next stop would be *America*.

45

Confident Shoes
Trusting the Captain

In the midst of the tempest, we
realized that we were going backwards.
From Lisbon to Philadelphia
December 22, 1943–January 7, 1944

There were 13 passengers on board the *Saint Thomé*, a
Portuguese freighter. Included in these were a Portuguese
couple, an American man, a German family with three
children—who were prisoners of war—and our family of five.
Since we knew German, we were able to converse with this
family and became quite friendly with them.

The crew was small and, to my dismay, didn't include a
doctor. With Mary just a few weeks away from her due date,
I made it a point to talk to the man in charge of the dispensary. "Could you deliver a baby should my wife go into labor?" I asked.

His reply was anything but reassuring. "Frankly," he said, "I don't have a clue as to what to do."

By now I was an experienced father, but by no means a doctor. I wouldn't have wanted to deliver a baby on dry land, let alone in the middle of an ocean. I also wondered what nationality a child, born at sea, might claim.

On Christmas Day the ship stopped moving. Apparently there were motor problems that needed remedying, so the motor was shut down for repairs. It seemed strange to be just riding the waves. It illustrated a life adrift without purpose or direction.

A day or so later the old freighter began to advance slowly. When the captain and first mate came for dinner, we questioned them. They honestly admitted that there were still some problems, but assured us that we need not fear. They knew what to do.

A large dinner was served at midnight on New Year's Eve, but we chose not to attend. We were quite satisfied with our cramped little cabin with only two bunks. Philip and Joanne slept on a bench and Buddy on the floor. The ship had taken a southern route so, thankfully, the children could spend New Year's Day playing on a sunny deck, which they had to themselves as the other passengers were sleeping in.

A few days later, as we neared the American coast, the ship turned northward. The sunshine faded into a steady rain, while clouds darkened and hung angrily overhead, stirring up wind and lightning. The ship leaned from side to side, creaking and twisting as if the waves and wind were tearing it apart. Then, in the midst of the tempest, we realized that we were going backwards. What could be going on? Feelings of panic began to well up in the passengers.

We needn't have worried, however, because this Captain, who had weathered many a storm, had simply ordered a change of course. Was it because of the weather or because of the war? None of us passengers knew. Years later we learned that three out of ten ships went down in those waters.

At lunchtime I was walking down the hall toward the dining room when the refrigerator doors broke loose. By the time I entered the room, food was sliding all over the floor. The place, though empty of people, appeared to be in shambles. It also appeared that I was one of the only passengers who'd still maintained a ravenous appetite. I took hold of the cabinet-sized radio to steady myself, then decided I might as well turn it on. Into the chaos around me triumphant singing blasted out:

> "The cross, it standeth fast. Hallelujah,
>   Hallelujah,
> Defying every blast, Hallelujah, Hallelujah,
> The winds of hell have blown; the world its
>   hate has shown,
> Yet it is not over-thrown, hallelujah for the
>   Cross.
> Hallelujah, Hallelujah, Hallelujah for the Cross
> Hallelujah, Hallelujah, Hallelujah for the
>   Cross."
>   —Horatius Bonar

What a feast for the soul.

As the frenzy of the sea calmed down, we resumed our original direction and finally reached the Philadelphia harbor. All of us, especially Mary, sighed with relief.

As soon as the gangplank was put out, the FBI and emigration officers came on board. They were primarily interested in the prisoners who, in the course of the voyage, had become our friends. Desiring to drop a few encouraging words as we walked by, Mary spoke in German. Immediately the delegation on board ushered her to a separate room for interrogation.

Once they saw her passport and heard how she'd learned German, they released her, but poor Mary had an awful scare. It took her quite some time to stop shaking.

After clearing customs we took a taxi to the mission's headquarters, anticipating some warmth and rest. However, there might as well have been a sign in the window, "no room in the inn."

"We're full up here," we were told. "You might try the Traveler's Aid." That night we huddled together in a miserably cold room, but the next day the Lord led us to the Baptist Institute where we were given a warm and cozy room.

By then, concern about our empty pockets was causing my spirits to fall to dangerous levels. Mary, though, feeling released from the dungeon and enjoying a warm fire, was as cheerful as a lark. "We're this far," she said. "Look at all God's done for us."

For a time I obstinately remained somber and morose, as we often tend to be in the valley between battles. "The Lord is good, a refuge in times of trouble. He cares for those who trust in Him," Mary went on.

Eventually her spirit of thanksgiving won over mine. Who can resist a *Mama Mbote?* In a short while a happy spirit came over each member of the family. Together we sat, warm and contented in our cozy room.

The women at the Institute took an interest in Mary, bringing her underwear and stockings, and assured us that our lodging was taken care of. Mary was right. God does "care for those who trust in Him."

With one battle behind us, we soon faced another. Due to some clerical error, train tickets wired by our family in Oregon could not be released. There was nothing to do but wait and trust. A few days later, on January 13, funds came through. So did our tickets. By 8:20 that evening, we were on the train headed for Los Angeles.

The train, crowded to capacity with soldiers, was bustling with movement and noise. We kept to ourselves and watched the soldiers pull out their lunches. When several pulled out the meat and threw the bread on the floor of the train, we had to muster self-control not to speak or reach for the bread. How we would have appreciated that bread for our own children the previous week, not to speak of friends in Belgium who were eating one meal a day with soup from one or two potatoes, or our African children waiting for a few mouthfuls of anything. We had to remind ourselves that America is the land of abundance—and the land of waste.

Having to change trains in New Orleans, we had a little time to kill so we took the children for a walk. When passing a toy store, we stopped to let the children have a look. When Joanne, not yet two, saw all the toys and especially the dolls, she raised her arms and exclaimed, "America, America, America." Looking at each other, we realized she was expressing the wonder and mixed feelings of us all.

46

Glossy Shoes Polished With Patience

Our baby was due...how I would have liked to fire up the train's engine.

Crossing America
1944

Why is it that when we are in a hurry, train wheels turn so slowly? We were anxious to reach Louisiana where I hoped to make contact with my soldier brother Art, who was temporarily stationed there. Thankfully, there were few similarities between African and American trains, but how I would have liked to fire up the engines that couldn't seem to do any better than their ho-hum methodical rhythm.

When we reached Louisiana, we all got off the train. Mary walked the children while I made phone call after phone call, none of which put me in contact with my kid brother. *Should I risk staying over in Louisiana?* I wondered. I did so want to see him. But this would mean finding a place to stay for the family, and our baby was due any time. *Perhaps brother Art has already moved on,* I thought, trying to console myself as I helped the family back onto the train.

The children sat by the windows taking in the sights while we sat back half-dozing. All of a sudden we were jolted awake with, "There's our palm trees!" The yell had come from our Philip; he had caught sight of some palm trees. The palm tree, from the day we first set foot on African soil, had achieved the status of favored tree and symbolized home. It was *our* tree.

By this time we were in Arizona and those palm trees seemed to wave a welcome to the African family passing by. When the train finally pulled into the Los Angeles station at 10:30 on the eighteenth of January, sister Kathryn and husband Arthur Bestvater were there waiting for us. They scooped us up and brought us to their home where, after baths, we collapsed. By now Mary was fighting a bad cold and Joanne had a fever.

After a few days of rest we took the daylight train to Fresno, where a whole delegation had come to meet us. We were thrilled and excited to see my parents. Looking into their faces we saw lines that the years had traced, but also a softer mellowness, the effect of the polishing of grace. To us, they were better looking than ever before. Then there were the twins Ruth and Esther, with their husbands, looking most happy. On some faces shock was ill-concealed—a grim reminder of our shabby appearance—and that we hadn't informed them that baby number four was coming. Mary hadn't had the opportunity to shop for maternity clothes and even her best cotton dress was becoming more ragged by the minute.

Once the initial shock was over, however, we melted together. Celebrating continued the next day when the family gave Mary a surprise birthday party and presented her with a new dress.

On Sunday I was asked to speak in church, which after the experience of our previous furlough, I should have declined. This time my emotions were stirred more than ever. The world seems so poorly balanced. While Europe was suffering the ravages of war, I was sitting in a quiet church listening to beautiful organ music amidst elegantly clad people.

But soon my heart was lifted in praise as I joined in the singing. How thankful I was to know that similar songs of praise were being sung on other shores, and that someday, there'll be a great gathering of the redeemed from every tribe and tongue and nation. When that day comes, we won't notice clothes and buildings; the face of our Redeemer will outshine all.

The following day the family insisted that Mary see a doctor. He and the family urged her to stay in Reedley for the birth of the baby, but this time my easygoing Mary put her foot down. "I'm going home to Mama," she insisted.

We decided it best to warn the family in Oregon of what they could expect in order to avoid the type of shock we'd imposed on our family in California. "We want to warn you that we're expecting another baby," Mary said shyly.

"Mary, you aren't! When is the baby due?"

"Next week!"

"You're kidding, Mary. You'd better hurry on over here."

"Yes, we're coming tomorrow!" Mary said and abruptly hung up.

After living without a telephone for six years, one feels self-conscious talking into a box—with or without shocking information to relate.

On January 28 sister Esther put us on the train to Salem, but before we reached our destination, we stopped over in Albany where sisters Emma and Eva were waiting. We had a few brief moments with them before the train continued to

Salem. By that time Mary was apprehensive and even considered hiding. She need not have worried, however. Elizabeth and Anna were prepared, and there was Mama. Mary flew into her arms and wept with joy.

The doctor advised Mary to rest and not go out the following week, a directive with which she was happy to comply with while her sisters took over the washing and the care of the family. She did allow herself one outing, which was the farewell of nephew Paul who was going off to the war. He would, in a short time, be hiding in the Belgian Ardennes and taking part in the Battle of the Bulge.

On February 11 Mary went into the Dallas hospital with a layette that had been sent to her from the women of the Baptist Institute in Philadelphia. Our son, Mark Andrew, was born a few minutes past midnight, making him our only non-contested American citizen and patriotically sharing the birthday of the notable president Abe Lincoln.

The birth went smoothly for Mary with no complications, except the discomfort of her bad cold. It had caused her to lose her voice and made her feel that she was contaminating all the babies in the hospital. Nevertheless, God had surely gone to a lot of trouble to bring her across the world in time to deliver in that hospital.

Several friends insisted that our baby should be named Abraham, after his father and in honor of Abe Lincoln, but Mary wouldn't hear of it. "One Abe in the family is enough," she said, so his name remained Mark.

47

Combat Boots on Decisive D Days

My thoughts...kept drifting to France.
Normandy, France
June 6, 1944—D Day

Gradually we settled into life in America, with the help of our family. A house was found where we could stay, but making it livable required a lot of work. By the time we had it all cleaned up, another, more suitable house was found. It too required almost as much work. My brother-in-law, Sam, had established a hardware store in Dallas called the Standard Supply. I helped out with various chores between speaking engagements in churches in the area, as well as at various functions such as a Gideon banquet and dinners for commercial clubs and other civic organizations. Buddy started school and adjusted remarkably well.

Our home church, the Dallas Mennonite Brethren, gave us a reception when we arrived; then continued to shower us with all kinds of home-canned fruits and vegetables. It was a delight to be enthusiastically welcomed by the pastor, George Janzen, who'd recently stepped into the pastorate. He had been one of our close friends from Biola. My mind flashed back to those days following my conversion. I remembered that he'd been among the first of a number of young people from around Dallas to attend Biola, setting an example for many, including me. In my mind's eye I saw him singing in a male quartet while his fiancée Mary chitchatted with my sister Kathryn.

Now George was a full-fledged pastor, while also championing the cause of world missions. As we settled into Dallas, George and Mary encouraged and affirmed us in our calling. What a blessing they were to us as they ministered to our emotional and spiritual needs.

In the years to follow they were to set another outstanding example. While pastoring a congregation and praying for 12 missionary volunteers, he and Mary came to realize that they were the ones who were to complete the number. They left their comfortable pastorate to go to Germany. There they trained nationals.

Our family was beginning to adjust to life in Dallas when, on April 6, we received a telegram telling us that Dad had suffered a stroke and asking me to come. The following day I said good-bye to Mary and boarded the train for Reedley, via Fresno. I knew it would be hard for her to be alone with the children for an undetermined time, but I was confident that family and friends would look after her.

When I arrived in Reedley, I found Dad paralyzed on one side and unable to talk. It was a hard time for Mother. I was glad to be part of the family, sharing the pain of the barrier that had fallen between my parents. With sorrow and apprehension I departed to return to Dallas.

May was coming to a close when I reached my family in Dallas. "The war" was the main subject of most conversations. On June 6, 1944, we heard that the Allied troops had invaded France. I knew that brother Art, now a father of two children, was one of them.

Mary's Mama had invited us to dinner that evening, but my thoughts refused to concentrate on the table. They kept drifting to France, wondering about my brother Art. Six years had passed since I'd seen him. To my knowledge, he'd never openly stated his position regarding his relationship to Christ. *Is he a true believer?* I wondered. *Has He put his faith in Christ as his Savior? Will I ever see him again?* How I wished our paths had crossed in Louisiana. It would have been reassuring to discuss these things before his departure.

The news of D-Day reached the world and we prayed for Art. As the days passed with no news, I dared to hope that it meant good news. But on July 7 a wire came from sister Kathryn: "Art killed in action on June 6." He had been one of the many paratroopers shot down as they were falling from the sky.

My first concern was for Mother, already worn from concern over Dad. Now she was called to bear the loss of her 28-year-old son—the fourth son she was to mourn. Mother was strong, yet so fragile. Obviously this was a severe testing ground for her.

Meanwhile, I tried to come to terms with the loss of my brother Art. He seemed to fill my conscious and subconscious mind, yet my earthly eyes would never see him again. I pictured the thoughtful gifts he'd bought that last Christmas we were together; in my ears I heard his youthful voice— his laughter.

Why hadn't I taken the condition of his soul more seriously? Here I was a missionary giving my life for others while neglecting my blood brother. Like David, the composer of many psalms, I lifted my anguished soul and cried, "Would to God I had died instead of him."

One early morning, helpless to still the torment of my soul, I got up and knelt in prayer. Heedless of implications, words poured from my lips. "If You open before me a door to France, I'll be willing to go and I'll do my best to win a brother or sister in the place of Art."

God heard that prayer.

48

Changing Shoes
Over Shifting Sands

Changes were taking place around the world.
USA
1945

The war was now reaching a climax. Many changes were taking place around the world. New boundaries were being drawn up; governments were changing their strategies. A new generation was growing up. Inevitably these changes would also affect mission strategies and procedures.

At such times critical decisions must be made. Refusal to adapt to change can weaken effectiveness or limit advancement, while plunging recklessly into change without analyzing the history of past victories and defeats can lead to costly detours.

Christ entrusted missions into the hands of His disciples the day He left the earth and when He addressed them with a command: "Go into all the world and preach the gospel" (Mk. 16:15). These early disciples were not left without prior personalized, in-depth, and on-the-job-training by the Master Himself. Christ, the first missionary, had been sent by God the Father to planet Earth. He was the only perfect missionary. Love, humility, self-sacrifice, compassion, flawless character, discipline, loyalty, courage to stand up to hypocrites and false teachers, diligence, and dependence on the Father were but a few of the traits perfectly modeled by His life. His methods were clearly defined as He lived and walked with people, using Scripture, teaching through stories and daily experiences, touching the sick, the broken, the down-trodden, the addicted, ministering to children and discipling believers. His strategies were marked by the Divine and often the miraculous in response to faith. The end result of all His endeavors was glory to His Father.

To this initiating command various terms have been applied such as, The Great Commission, The Gospel Mandate, or The Global Endeavor. Personally, I prefer a title such as The Believer's Privilege. That God should allow *us* the *privilege* of cooperating with Him in such a magnificent project is beyond my comprehension. Each of Christ's followers or disciples is included. Every believer is a missionary. Some are chosen for distant places; others for their hometowns. Each generation is challenged to reach the world with the message of God's love and His power to transform lives.

To achieve this goal, in a changing world with an increasing population, it's only logical to seek the most effective means available to each generation. While implementing change, however, there are certain nonnegotiable strategies that must be heeded. God's work must always be done God's way, and the end result must always glorify God. When these strategies are bypassed, warning signals are set off with blaring lights. One danger lies in becoming so organized and structured that the effort becomes "big business." Little room is left for demonstrations of faith, prayer, or the miraculous. What spiritual results can we expect if we limit a supernatural God to our human schemes, or leave Him out of our carefully structured organizations? How easily we tend to rely on human wisdom and power to the exclusion of "Holy Spirit" power. Another danger is when organizations or denominations are promoted to the detriment of the gospel or the glory of God, especially when they compete against each other. But the greatest danger of all lies in the failure to model Christ in everyday life. Yielding daily to Christ and His sanctifying process is the secret to becoming an effective missionary. Nothing speaks louder than one's life. How we live is the greatest proof to a sinful world of the power of the gospel of grace. Through these unchanging elements we can view the necessary changes that must be implemented in order to adapt to a changing world.

In those years there were gradual changes as mission boards were becoming organized, requiring more specialization, and defining boundaries. We recognized that such changes were necessary and that they would not be without risks.

The Kafumba mission station, which was started by the Janzens and was where we spent our first term, was now officially under the auspices of the Mennonite Brethren Foreign Mission Society. Encouraged by this Board and our pastor, we also became formally affiliated with that Mission.

Since we had a particular burden for the very large Babunda tribe, we presented to the mission the possibility of opening a new mission station in the southern part of that tribe. to this they readily gave their assent, and Mary and I rejoiced.

While negotiations were going on, some family members and friends were facing us with other propositions, with our best interests at heart. They approached us with, "It's time to talk."

"We're listening," we replied.

"You need to face reality. There's Mary's health to consider. Aren't you concerned? She can't stand the tropics.

Look at all the sicknesses she's had. You've had your share too, Abe."

"Obviously you have a point," I replied.

"You haven't shirked your duty."

"I hope not."

"After two terms, you've accomplished a fair amount. It's time for you to think about raising your family. You owe it to your children. They need an education and the advantages of living in America."

"Yes, we've counted the cost to ourselves and to our children," I assured them.

"It could cost you a grave."

"Yes, we have come to terms with that."

"But what about us? Don't we count? We'll miss you. We worry about you. We won't get to see your children growing up. What about your parents? They need you now in their sunset years."

This last point hit hard. We loved our family dearly and didn't want to be the cause of unnecessary pain or difficulty. We had to recognize, however, that our "call" had implications of sacrifice and suffering on them as well. All we could do was pray that they might enter with us into the calling, and find joy in their own calling and involvement.

To many we seemed obstinate, hardheaded, unrealistic, and irresponsible. We couldn't blame people for thinking this way of us, or for their loving concern. If only we could explain the weight of responsibility we felt toward God or, in the terms of Paul the missionary: "Woe to me if I do not preach the gospel!" (1 Cor. 9:16). If only we could adequately describe the scenes that beckoned us. In a booklet, published by Back to the Bible Broadcast, we found a poem that expressed our hearts:

> If you had been to heathen lands
> Where weary souls stretch out their hands,
> To plead, yet no one understands,

Would you go back? Would you?
If you had seen the women bear
Their heavy loads with none to share,
Had heard them weep with none to care.
Would you go back? Would you?
If you had seen them in despair,
And beat their breasts and pull their hair
While demon powers filled the air,
Would you go back? Would you?
IF you had seen the glorious sight
When heathen people in their night
Were brought from darkness into light.
Would you go back? Would you?
Yet still they wait a weary throng,
They've waited, some so very long,
When shall despair be turned to song?
I'm going back! Would you?"

A strange peace and assurance comes when one knows that the right decision—the one that pleases God—has been made. Obedient hearts are joy-filled hearts. As we held our ground, first resignation and then a measure of that peace was given to our family. Though not without sorrow, they relinquished us and assured us that they would stand behind us and care for our parents. In the measure that God enabled our shoes to go, He enabled their shoes to stay. In the years ahead they'd prove God's calling in their own lives as they remained steadfast in love to us and in service to God. Together we were exercising our privilege in God's great enterprise of love. Together we will, some day, rejoice in the presence of our Master and share the reward He has promised.

49

Worn Shoes
Homeward Bound

We saw a bottle being passed around
a little too frequently in the cockpit.

Atlantic Ocean
New York USA to Freetown Sierra Leone
to Libreville Gabon
to Lagoz Nigeria
to Kinshasa—Kikwit—Kafumba, Zaïre
1945

After a year in America—what we called our homeland—
we found ourselves traveling home to Africa.

Stopping briefly in Reedley where there were more teary
farewells, we set out for New York. Carefully conserved gas
coupons proved quite sufficient for the trip. The Sudan Interior Mission headquarters provided lodging for our family
while we waited for a booking to Africa.

I wore out the office personnel at the steamship companies when, day after day, I inquired, "Any boat available?"

One good thing about these persistent visits was the opportunities to witness. Some listened, others openly classified me as a fanatic or fool for taking my family to Africa with a war hardly over, and for what purpose? "Why not leave the heathen alone? They're happy the way they are."

Sometimes such reasoning can be oppressing—until one turns to Heaven's descriptions: "For the message of the cross is foolishness to those who are perishing, but to us who are being saved it is the power of God" (1 Cor. 1:18). God's secret wisdom has been "revealed to us by His Spirit" (1 Cor. 2:10). Thus was it described by the apostle Paul, our early missionary hero.

Eventually I grew accustomed to negative answers to my inquiries about passage and had begun to adjust to the idea that my missionary activity was restricted to office workers at steamship companies. So I was shaken when informed that the Elder Depster line of England had a ship, the SS *Calgary*, that was bound for west Africa.

By now the children were enjoying their stay at the mission with the various guests. One of these guests was Mr. Howard, editor of *The Sunday School Times*. He would keep the children spellbound making all kinds of bird calls and describing habits of birds and other creatures. Dr. and Mrs. J. Sidlow Baxter were some other visitors we shall never forget.

The Baxters didn't know that meals were not served on Sunday so they were caught unprepared. Dr. Baxter secretly went out on Sunday morning to see if he could find a bread store open and returned with a loaf of bread. When Mrs. Baxter raised an eyebrow he said with a wink, "The Lord is not as particular in America as back home in England."

Without the pressure of a tight schedule, we had time to enjoy our children. Philip, now four, was at an age when he kept twisting his words. Since our room was on the eighth floor of the SIM building, he would often suggest enthusiastically, "Let's take the alligator." It reminded us of Buddy, who used to have a similar problem with words. One of these was *apricots*, which he kept calling "apple guts."

The children were also enjoying their fill of American foods, including the old American standby: peanut butter. During our travels we'd visited my aunt and uncle's farm in North Dakota, where we were served *greeve scmult*, or pork crackling butter. A neighbor's lad who'd spent the night there called out, "Pass the peanut butter please." When everyone laughed he said, "I don't care what you call it, it's good anyhow."

Our children would soon be looking into African kettles that included chicken entrails that looked like spaghetti, a large rat, grasshoppers, or worms. But tell an African that the white man eats frog's legs and it'll turn his stomach! Also, "Why," he'll ask, "would Jews not eat pork but raise pigs?" What a strange world.

The voyage on the SS *Calgary* was unusually good. This was due, in part, to fair weather, but also to the fact that the ship was heavily loaded with iron products and harbor equipment for Liberia, which filled the deck. The ship literally cut through the waves.

In conversing with the wireless operator one day, I mentioned the fact of man's inborn wickedness. His response to this was ridicule. "That's not in the Bible," he said and refused to look at the New Testament I pulled out of my pocket.

The next day we came to a small island where most of the crew went on shore. After a night of drinking and brawling, I hardly recognized this same man the next morning. His face was badly cut and swollen. When he saw me he immediately dropped his eyes. He knew only too well that "the heart is deceitful…and desperately wicked" (Jer. 17:9 KJV).

A major stop was Freetown in Sierra Leone. There the ship anchored out in the harbor and we were transferred to another ship. Once more we had to climb a rope ladder.

This ship carried practically no cargo but was loaded to capacity with soldiers, most of whom were Canadian officers. Mary and Joanne were the only women on board. It had some advantages for them as they were shown ever possible kindness and courtesy, but the poor ship bobbed about on top of the waves like a cork, and most of those soldiers suffered from violent seasickness. They lay about on the decks in great discomfort. Having good sea legs myself, I was not able to sympathize with them as Mary could.

When the crew was informed that a missionary was on board, they organized a Sunday morning service to be held on deck and asked me to speak. I was surprised that almost all the passengers on board showed up and enthusiastically participated in choosing hymns. Their hearty singing wouldn't fit the category of a men's choir, but how it lifted my soul. These were men who'd seen the grim realities of war. Heaven was still high on their priorities.

We were still at sea on September 2, 1945, when word came through that the war was officially over. The gunner crew started dumping overboard large metal boxes filled with ammunition. Considering possible uses for those metal boxes, I asked if I might have a couple. They kindly gave me two, which later became excellent bug-proof book boxes for my mobile bookstore.

When we arrived at the port of Libreville in the Gabon, we had quite a wait for still another ship to take us to Lagos. We stayed at a French mission house where the children got sick from eating overripe mangoes they'd picked up from the ground.

We took a walk to the mission cemetery and read the inscriptions on the tombstones. We noticed, by the dates, that most of the missionaries laid to rest there were young. Challenged by their example we knelt down, once again, and committed ourselves to God—for life or death.

The ship we boarded in Libreville was a log-carrier loaded, this time, with many African soldiers returning home from the war. After finding our cabin and bringing in our baggage, the boys and I went to a porthole to watch the loading operation. An African lad walking by stopped to chat with us. The subject of our conversation soon turned to the gospel of God's love, to which he not only showed interest, but expressed immediate acceptance.

The dinner bell rang and Bud and I turned to go, while Philip stayed at the porthole. Suddenly he turned around crying inconsolably, "Mummy, Daddy, they've killed our native," he screamed.

The crew had been trying out the rigging and hoist. Our lad had been standing, a minute ago, just below the radar equipment when the boom pole swung out and crushed his head.

We were all sad that day, but thankful that our young friend was safe in Heaven. It was an object lesson for deep conversation in our family that day. How kind of God to lead us to this particular lad who urgently needed to make his destiny sure. How we wondered at his eagerness and readiness, and how happy we could be that we would see him again.

At Lagos we boarded a plane heading for Kinshasa.[1] We became alarmed when we saw a bottle being passed around a little too frequently in the cockpit. So we weren't surprised when we learned that we'd overshot our destination and had to turn back.

The words of the song "Safe in the Arms of Jesus" were never more sweet in the air, and never were we more happy to set feet on the ground.

Before leaving the airport our little Joanne became violently ill; probably from some palm nuts or impure water. Some Catholic sisters, who were nurses, were waiting in the airport. When they saw our predicament they came over to

---

1.   Then Léopoldville

ask if they could help. They picked up Joanne, carried her to their own car, and rushed her to a dispensary nearby. There they cared for her dehydrated condition. Once again we lifted our hearts in praise to God our Father for sending two angels in the nick of time.

It seemed like a dream when we finally reached Kikwit and then Kafumba. Seeing our fellow missionaries and friends was a homecoming indeed. A few days later we received a telegram from the homeland saying that my Dad in Reedley had gone home—to glory. When our son Philip heard the news he said, "Then Grampa got there before we did."

"Yes, Philip," I assured him. "Grampa got there before us, but we're coming too."

Following such conversations one cannot help but sigh and wish to be at the end of life's journey and in that happy place where there is no sighing and sadness; no violence, crime, and witchcraft, no fear and pain, no hate, heartache, sorrow, or disappointment.

Meanwhile, we must keep trekking the dusty paths of life until our call comes to cross the last river that takes us to our final home. For us, many exciting and traumatic twists and turns lay ahead that would make those of the past almost dull in comparison.